TISSI
TYPE

* Diese drei Alphabete hat Rosmarie Tissi mit Reissfeder und Tusche konstruiert. (1972, 1973 und 1975 gab es noch keine Computer für Grafik). Später hat sie die Buchstaben digitalisiert. Die weiteren Schriften sind alle digital entstanden. Mit Céline Odermatt, Font Designerin bei Lineto, hat Tissi die für den ganzen Schriftsatz der Sinaloa erforderlichen 200 Sonderzeichen definiert. Die Sinaloa ist bei Lineto erhältlich.

---

* Rosmarie Tissi constructed these three alphabets with a drawing pen and ink. (1972, 73 and 75 computers for design did not exist). Later, she digitalized the letters. The following alphabets were created digitally. Together with Céline Odermatt, the font designer of Lineto, Tissi defined the 200 special characters required for the entire Sinaloa typesetting. Sinaloa is available at Lineto.

Weitgereiste Alphabete

Rosmarie Tissi ist seit Jahrzenten eine feste Grösse in der internationalen Gestaltungsszene und steht seit jeher für aussergewöhnliche Spitzenleistungen in der Tradition der Schweizer Grafik. Fast 40 Jahre war sie der eine Teil der bekannten Ateliergemeinschaft Odermatt & Tissi, von 1968 bis zu Sigi Odermatts Tod 2017. Die Entwürfe entstanden in einem einzigen Atelierraum, „ohne Mitarbeiter und ohne Maschinen", wie es einmal hiess. Dabei arbeitete jeder an seinen eigenen Aufträgen, lediglich Anmerkungen, Vorschläge oder Änderungsideen wurden auf einem grossen Tisch in der Mitte ausgetauscht. Vielleicht liegt das Erfolgsgeheimnis dieser speziellen Partnerschaft gerade in der Unterschiedlichkeit der Charaktere und der Arbeitsweisen. Für Odermatt bestand die Grundidee stets im strikten Raster, auf dem alles aufgebaut wurde. Dagegen stehen für Tissi Experiment und Spontaneität im Vordergrund, „das sind meine italienischen Wurzeln", die strenge Ordnung kommt erst in der Folge dazu. Und während der eine mit dem idyllischen Standort in Zürich vollauf zufrieden gewesen ist, seine Wohnung befand sich sogar im gleichen Haus, lockte die andere stets die Ferne, das Fremde und Exotische.

Mehr als 70 Länder auf 6 Kontinenten bereiste Rosmarie Tissi im Lauf der Zeit – meistens fernab der Touristenströme und immer allein. „Man muss dann nicht Rücksicht auf die Mitreisenden nehmen und kann einfach entscheiden, wie und wohin es weitergeht." Sie brauche diese Ausbrüche, die Suche nach neuen Anregungen und Konfrontation mit dem Unbekannten. So verliess sie immer wieder die konzentrierte Atelierarbeit und startete ins Abenteuer, zwischen zwei und vier Monate war sie unterwegs, häufig in exotischen Regionen und oftmals zu unvorhergesehenen Zielen. „Wenn ich daran zurückdenke, was ich auf mich genommen habe, um überhaupt dahin zu kommen…"

Die Ernte dieser extremen Expeditionen umfasst nicht nur zahllose, teils faszinierende, teils wunderliche Erinnerungsstücke sowie eine Reihe ebenso stabiler wie handlicher Koffer als ihre wechselnden Begleiter. Denn in der Folge dieser ausgedehnten Touren entstanden wiederholt Schriftentwürfe. Die erste dieser eigenwilligen Alphabete entstand 1972 und wurde im Rahmen eines Letraset-Wettbewerbs auch gleich ins Programm aufgenommen. Die Abreibebuchstaben waren seinerzeit unerlässliches Gestaltungsmittel in vielen Grafikateliers, entsprechend gross war ihre Verbreitung. „Dafür gab es herzlich wenig Geld, aber darum ging es ja nicht."

Diese „Sinaloa" getaufte Schrift – „damals gab es das berüchtigte Drogenkartell von El Chapo natürlich noch nicht" – sollte sich als ausgesprochener Longseller erweisen. Rosmarie Tissi begegnete ihr auf den Reisen immer wieder, auf Plakaten, Werbezetteln und in Zeitschriften… und das selbst in entlegenen Regionen. „In Australien sass ich einmal beim Coiffeur und habe in einem Magazin gleich mehrere Inserate mit meiner Sinaloa gesehen."

Noch in den 1970er-Jahren schuf Rosmarie Tissi weitere Alphabete als Folgen der Fernreisen. Druckschriftenentwurf war damals noch echte „Handarbeit", Grafikerinnen, die sich damit auseinandersetzten, bildeten die grosse Ausnahme. Umso beachtlicher, wie viele Alphabete schliesslich im Zürcher Atelier entstanden, natürlich immer mit entsprechend exotischen Titeln. Man braucht schon einen sehr guten Atlas, um die ursprünglichen Namensgeber verorten zu können: Sonora (1972), Mindanao (1975), Palawan (2014), Sarawak (2019), Siladen (2020), Lombok (2021), Sabah (2021), Vanuatu (2021), Roatan (2022), Ponape (2022).

Dabei ist zu beachten, dass die Charaktere keineswegs folkloristische oder regionaltypische Bezüge haben. Fernöstliche oder mittelamerikanische Elemente wird man vergeblich suchen. Es handelt sich viel eher jeweils um ein Destillat aus den Entdeckungen, Erfahrungen und Erinnerungen, die Rosmarie Tissi gerade an diesen Orten oder Gebieten gesammelt hat und die sie an ihren Zeichentisch begleitet haben. Das rätselhaft Fremdländische verbindet sich zudem mit der strengen Schweizer Typografie zu den unverwechselbaren Tissi-Alphabeten. Die Exotik der Bezeichnungen unterstreicht zugleich die markante Eigenständigkeit und wird zum Markenzeichen – mit einem hintergründigen Lächeln der Eingeweihten.

Nur einmal ist die Grafikerin von dieser exotischen Nomenklatur abgewichen: Denn die Schrift TA|TE basiert auf dem Entwurf für die Creation Gallery in Tokio. Diese lud alljährlich internationale Designer zur Gestaltung eines Objekts ein, das dann zugunsten von UNICEF verkauft wurde.

Firmennamen aus zwei Inseraten in einem australischen Magazin.

Ladenbeschriftung in Kuching, Sarawak, ein Bundesstaat Malaysias auf Borneo.

2007 hiess das vorgegebene Objekt „Cup and Saucer" (Tasse/Teller) Tissi beschriftete die Tasse mit ENJOY. Aus diesen fünf Buchstaben entwickelte sie anschliessend das komplette Alphabet TA|TE (2010).

Abgesehen von TA|TE entstanden alle Alphabete ohne konkreten Anlass. Das hatte auch ökonomische Gründe. Denn nach den langen Atelier-Pausen fehlten erst einmal neue Aufträge, so blieb Zeit, sich diesen kreativen Fingerübungen zu widmen, auch, um neue Gestaltungswege zu erproben. Wobei nicht zu vergessen ist, dass das Komponieren einer kompletten Schrift ebenso komplexe wie diffizile Arbeit bedeutet. Denn das Zusammenspiel der einzelnen Lettern muss in jeder Kombination funktionieren, dazu kommt eine Vielzahl von Sonderzeichen, diakritischen Elementen und Ziffern. Ganz abgesehen davon, dass das Ergebnis natürlich „aus einem Guss" sein muss. Die Digitalisierung hat hier einiges erleichtert, doch die Feinarbeit bleibt – der Teufel steckt bekanntlich im Detail und nirgends wird das so deutlich wie in der Typografie!

Nach Odermatts Tod und der Auflösung des Ateliers kam die glückliche Verbindung von Reiseabenteuer und Schriftentwurf erst einmal zum Erliegen. Zunächst musste die Studiokatze versorgt werden, und danach – „der Koffer war schon gepackt" – kam das Covid 19-Virus mit Lockdown und Beschränkungen. Das bedeutete nicht nur den Verzicht auf jegliche Reise, sondern auch auf die meisten persönlichen wie beruflichen Kontakte. Aber aus Enttäuschung und Frustration wurde bald trotzige Aktivität: „Dann mache ich halt wieder einmal eine Schrift!"

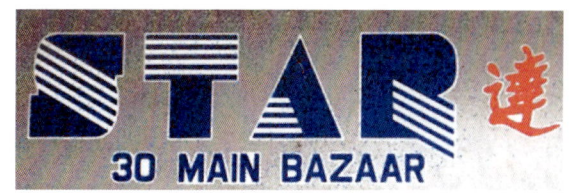

Drei neue Alphabete sollten es ursprünglich werden, inzwischen sind fünf während der Corona-Zwangspause entstanden. Mittlerweile sind auch die Arbeiten an allen Sonderzeichen abgeschlossen – „das Pfund-Zeichen hat mich geärgert…" Die Namenswahl mit lange zurückliegenden Reisen zeigt das ungebrochene Fernweh. Doch die Erlebnisse und Erinnerungen sind so lebendig und aussergewöhnlich wie die daraus gewonnenen Buchstaben.

Herbert Lechner

Well-traveled alphabets

Rosmarie Tissi has been a fixture on the international design scene for decades and has always stood for exceptional excellence in the tradition of Swiss graphic design. For almost 40 years, she was one part in the well-known Odermatt & Tissi studio partnership, from 1968 until Sigi Odermatt's death in 2017. Their designs were created in a single studio room, "without employees and without machines," as it was once put. Each of them worked on their own commissions, with only notes, suggestions and ideas for changes being exchanged on a large table in the middle. Perhaps the secret to the success of this special partnership lies precisely in the differences between the characters and their working methods. For Odermatt, the starting point was always the strict grid on which everything was built. For Tissi, on the other hand, experimentation and spontaneity are in the foreground, "those are my Italian roots," and the strict order comes only later. And while Odermatt was completely content with the idyllic location in Zurich—his apartment was even in the same house—Tissi has always been lured by the distant, the foreign and exotic.

Over the course of time, Rosmarie Tissi has traveled to more than 70 countries on six continents—mostly far away from the tourist crowds and always on her own. "You then don't have to take fellow travelers into consideration and can simply decide how and where to go next." She needs these escapes, the search for new stimuli, and the confrontation with the unknown. So time and again she left the focused studio work and launched into adventure, spending between two and four months on the road, frequently in far-flung places and often to unforeseen destinations. "When I think back to all the things I took on to get there in the first place..."

The harvest of these extreme expeditions comprises not only countless souvenirs—partly fascinating, partly whimsical—and a series of equally sturdy and handy suitcases as her changing companions. For in the wake of these extended tours, she repeatedly created typeface designs, too. The first of these idiosyncratic alphabets was designed in 1972. It was selected in a Letraset competition and immediately included in the company's typeface library. At the time, rub-down letters were an indispensable design tool in many graphic design studios, and the distribution of the typefaces was correspondingly vast. "There was precious little money for it, but that wasn't the point."

This typeface, christened "Sinaloa"—"at that time, of course, El Chapo's notorious drug cartel did not yet exist"—was to prove a long seller. On her travels, Rosmarie Tissi encountered it again and again, on posters, advertising slips and in magazines... and even in remote regions. "In Australia I was once sitting at the hairdresser's and saw several ads featuring my Sinaloa all in one magazine."

Still in the 1970s, Rosmarie Tissi created more alphabets as a result of her long-distance travels. At that time, typeface design was still real manual work, and women who tackled it were the great exception. It's all the more remarkable how many alphabets she eventually created in the Zurich studio, always with correspondingly exotic titles, of course. One needs a very good atlas to be able to locate the original namesakes: Sonora (1972), Mindanao (1975), Palawan (2014), Sarawak (2019), Siladen (2020), Lombok (2021), Sabah (2021), Vanuatu (2021), Roatan (2022), Ponape (2022).

It should be noted that the typefaces have no folkloric or regional references whatsoever. One will look in vain for Far Eastern or Central American elements. It is much more a distillation of the discoveries, experiences, and memories that Rosmarie Tissi gathered in these places that have accompanied her to her drawing table. Also, the enigmatically foreign combines with the strict Swiss typography to create the unmistakably Tissi alphabets. At the same time, these traveler's designations underscores Tissi's striking independence, and becomes a trademark—with a cryptic smile for those in the know.

Only once did Tissi deviate from her geographic nomenclature, for the typeface TA|TE, which is based on a design for the Creation Gallery in Tokyo. Every year, the gallery invited international designers to design an object that would then be sold to benefit UNICEF. In 2007, the theme was called "Cup and Saucer". Tissi labeled the cup with ENJOY. From these five letters she subsequently developed the complete TA|TE alphabet (2010).

T-shirt print VIVA VILA,
Vila, the capital of Vanuatu, former New Hebrides.

Running shirt READY TO RUN
a specialty shop for running items in Austin Texas.

With the exception of TA|TE, none of the title typefaces was created for a specific purpose. There were also economic reasons for this. After the long hiatuses from the studio work, there were no new commissions, so Tissi had time to devote herself to these creative exercises, also to try out new ways of designing. It should not be forgotten that composing a complete typeface is just as complex as it is difficult. The interaction of the individual letters must function in every combination, and there is also a multitude of special characters, diacritical elements, and numerals. Not to mention the fact that the result must of course be "cut from the same cloth". Digitization has made things easier here, but the need to apply the finishing touches remains—as we all know, the devil is in the details, and nowhere is this more evident than in typography!

After Odermatt's death and the dissolution of the studio, the happy combination of travel adventure and type design came to a halt. First, the studio cat had to be taken care of, and then—"the suitcase was already packed"—the Covid-19 virus arrived, with a lockdown and other restrictions. This meant not only the renunciation of any travel plans, but disappointment and frustration soon turned into defiant activity: "Well, I'll do another typeface then!"

The original plan foresaw three new alphabets. Eventually Tissi has created five during the forced Covid break. In the meantime, she completed work on all special characters, too—"the pound sign annoyed me…" The names chosen after long past travels shows the unbroken wanderlust, but the experiences and memories are as vivid and extraordinary as the letterforms derived from them.

Herbert Lechner

Signet und Plakat für das
Theater 11 in Zürich,
mit der „11" (negativ) aus
dem Alphabet Sinaloa.

Logo and poster for
Theater 11 in Zürich, with
the "11" (negative) from
the alphabet Sinaloa.

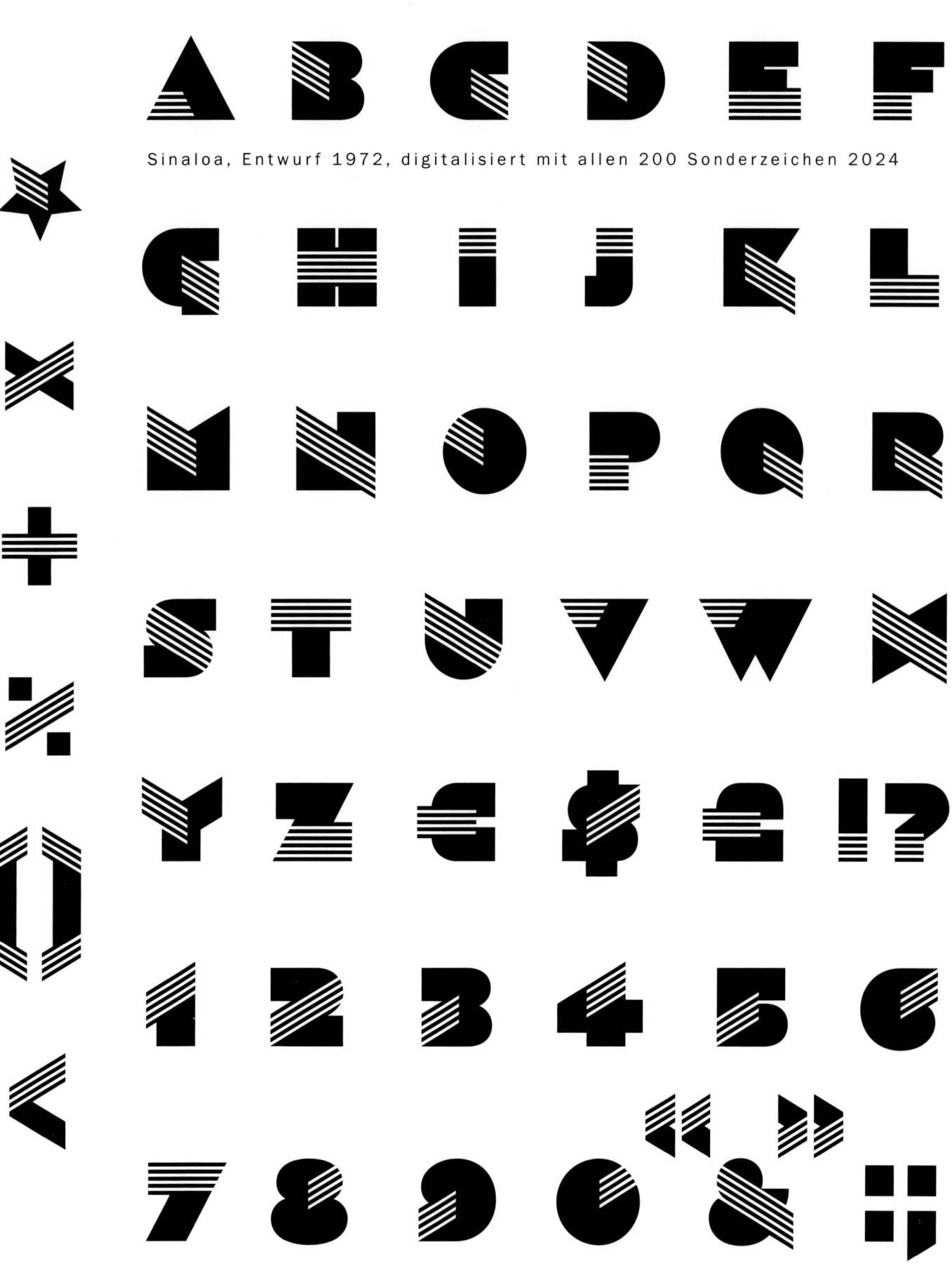
Sinaloa, Entwurf 1972, digitalisiert mit allen 200 Sonderzeichen 2024

Sonora, Entwurf 1972, digitalisiert 2022

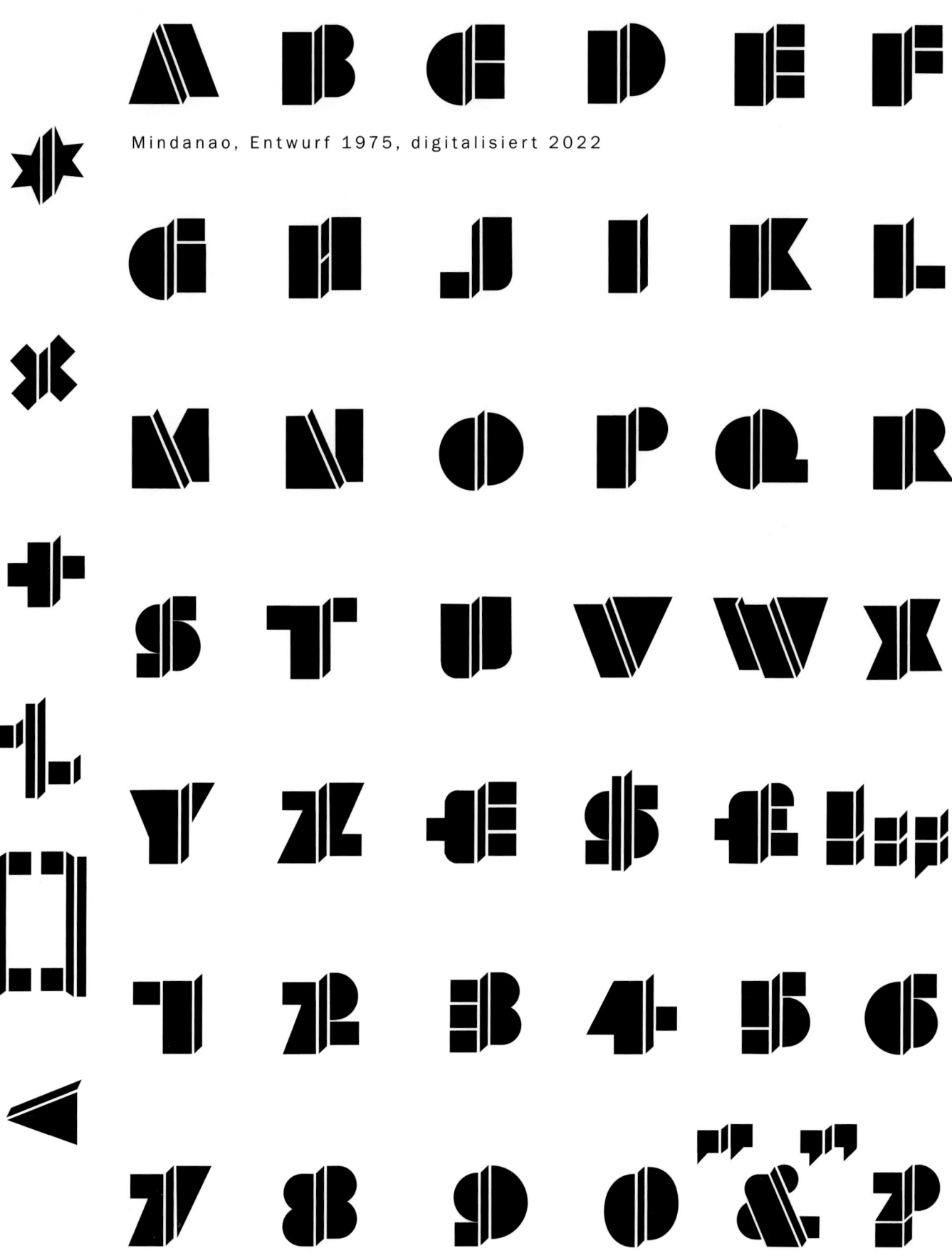
Mindanao, Entwurf 1975, digitalisiert 2022

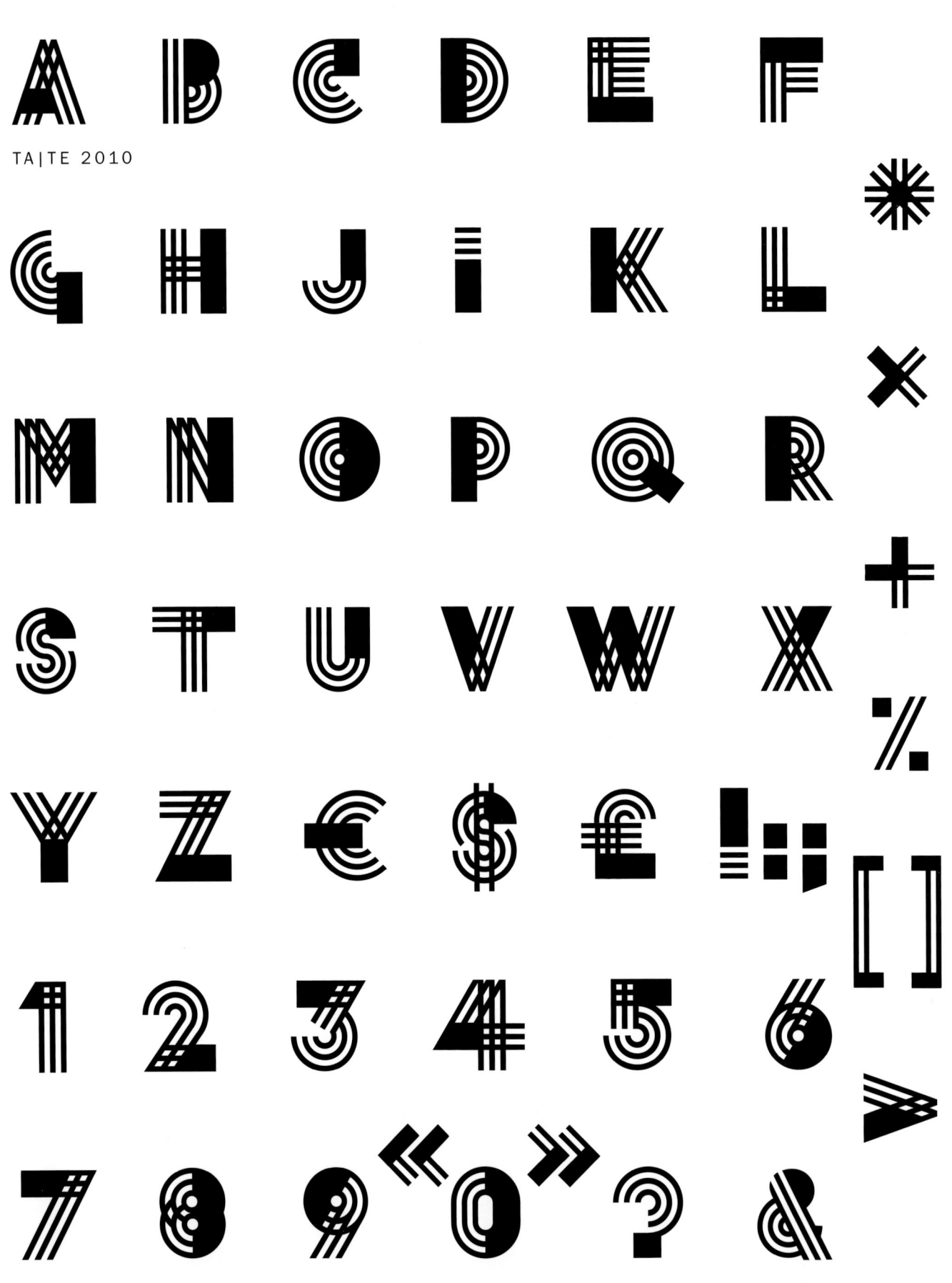

TA|TE 2010

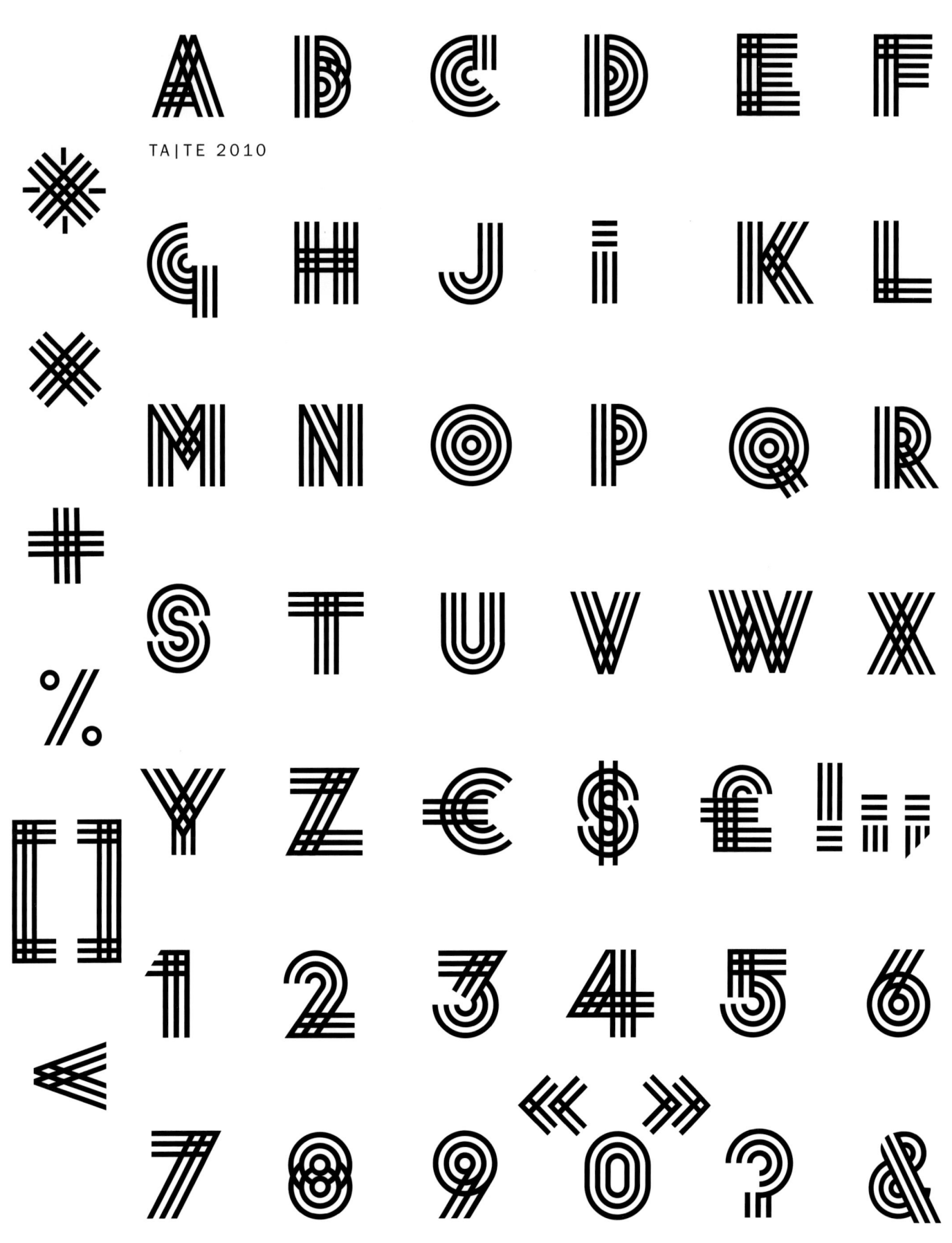

TA|TE 2010

Ausstellung „Rosmarie Tissi-Graphic Design" in der Art Gallery der Central Michigan Universität, mit Buchstaben aus Palawan und TA|TE.

Exhibition "Rosmarie Tissi-Graphic Design" at the Art Gallery of Central Michigan University, with letters from Palawan and TA|TE.

Für die geplante Ausstellung während des AGI Kongresses in Neuseeland, 2023, wurden die AGI Mitglieder eingeladen, ein Plakat zu gestalten mit nur zwei Worten, weiss auf schwarzem Grund.

For the planned exhibition during the AGI Congress in New Zealand 2023, the AGI members were invited to create a poster with only two words, white on black.

Beitrag zum Tasse/Teller Projekt der Creation Gallery in Tokio. 2007

Contribution to the cup and saucer project promoted by the Creation Gallery, Tokyo. 2007

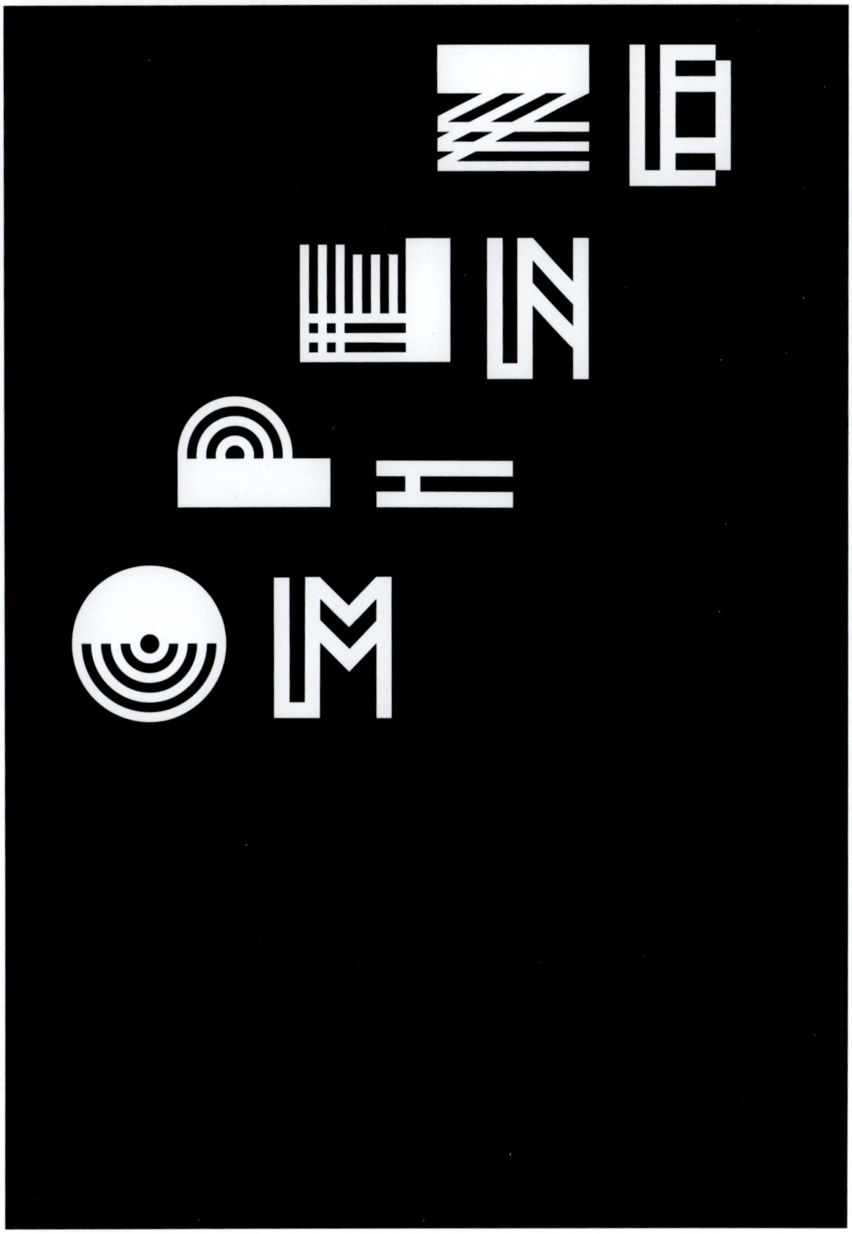

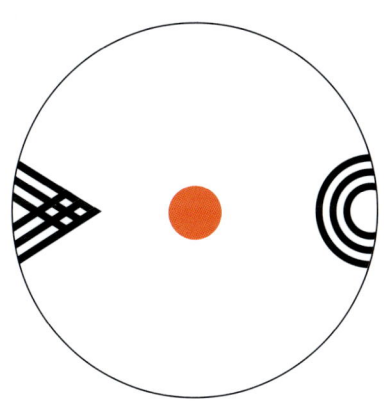

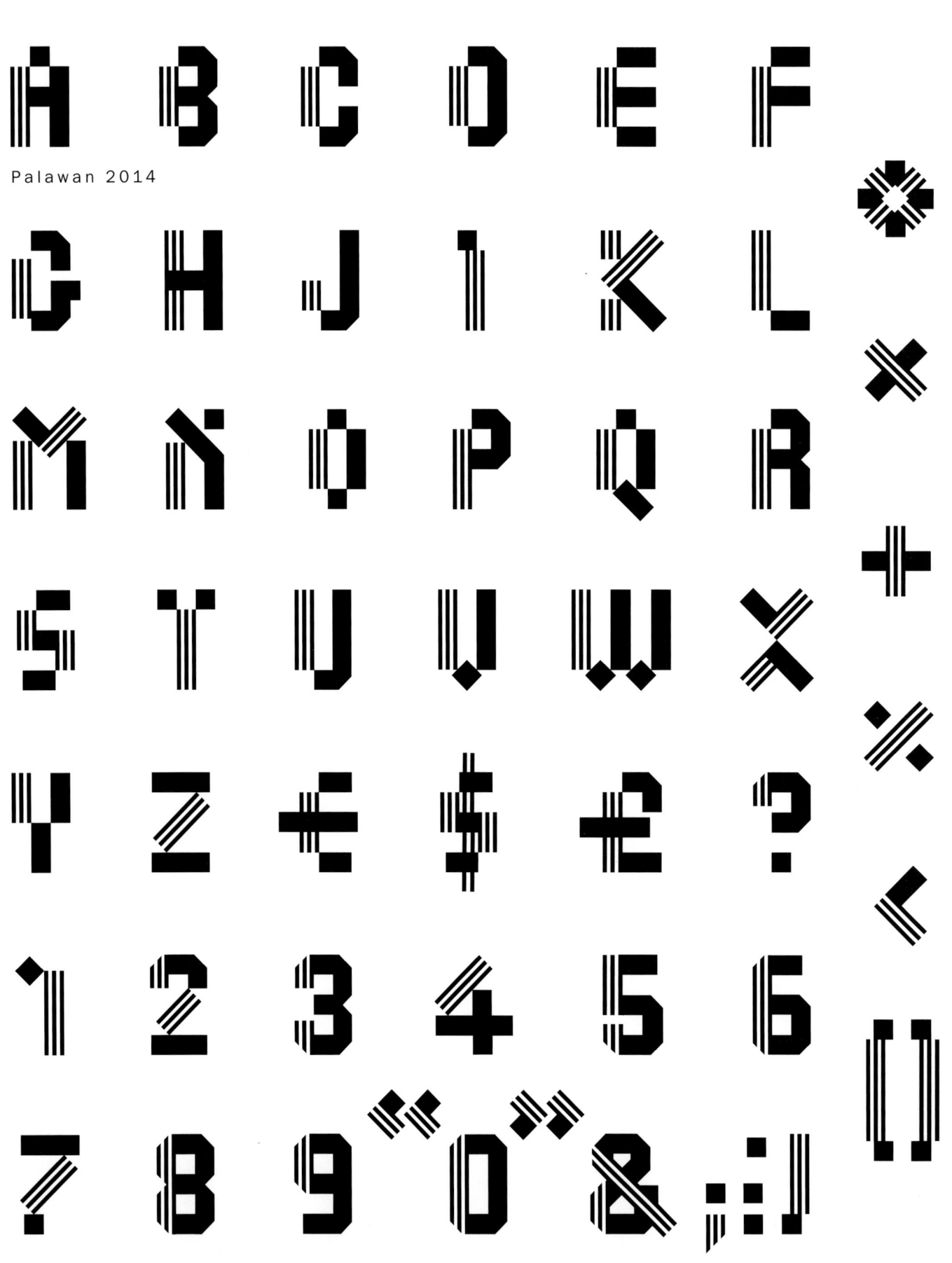

Ausstellung „Anni Albers, Elaine Lustig Cohen und Rosmarie Tissi" in der Pratt Manhattan Gallery, New York. Plakat mit Buchstaben aus den Alphabeten Palawan, Mindanao und, leicht verändert, Sinaloa. 2018

Exhibition "Anni Albers, Elaine Lustig Cohen and Rosmarie Tissi" at the Pratt Manhattan Gallery, New York. Poster with letters from the typefaces Palawan, Mindanao and, slightly changed, Sinaloa. 2018

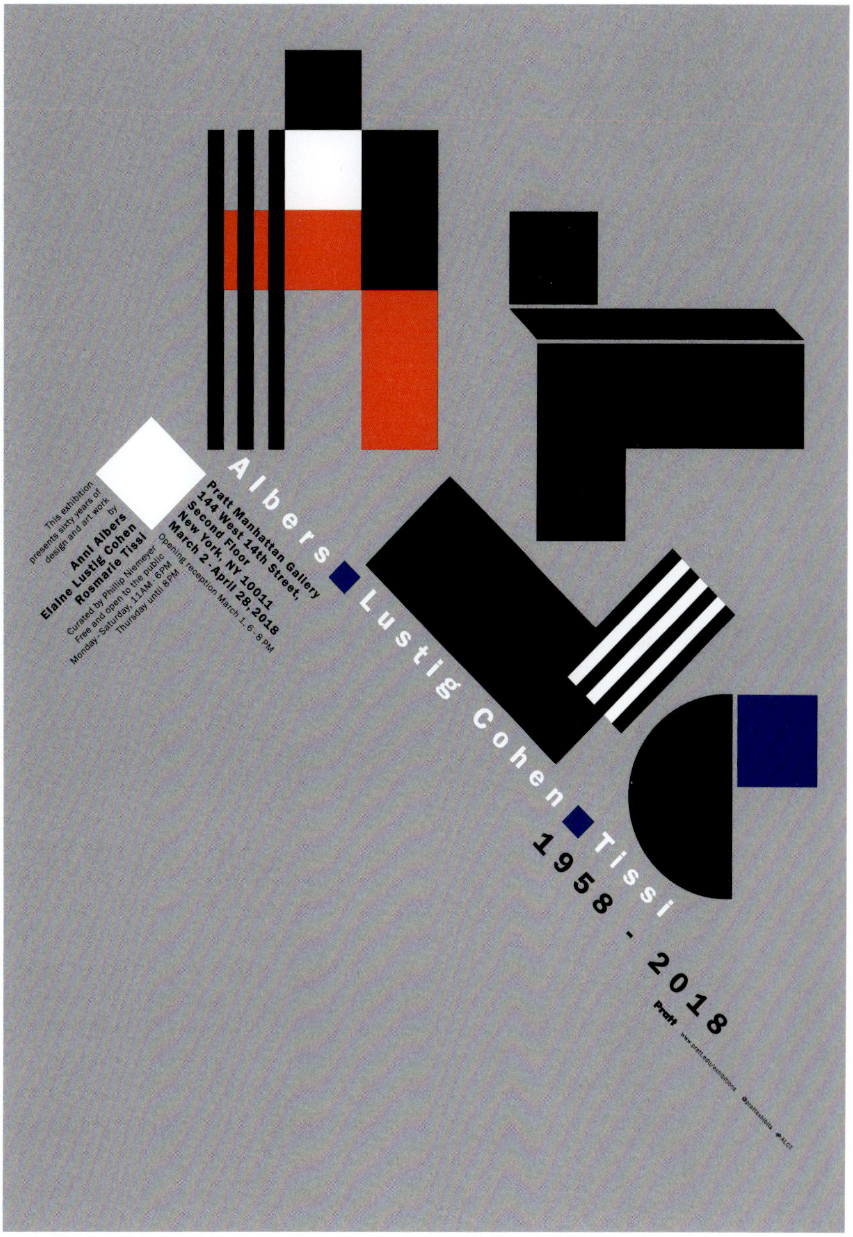

Deckblatt eines Kalenders für eine Druckerei 40 × 60 cm. 2020 in römischen Ziffern MMXX mit Palawan Buchstaben.

Cover of a calendar for a printing firm 40 × 60 cm. 2020 in roman figures MMXX with Palawan letters

Entwurf zum Plakat für das 31. Schaffhauser Jazzfestival 2020. Mit Buchstaben aus dem TA|TE Alphabet. 2019

Proposal for the poster for the 31th Jazzfestival held in Schaffhausen 2020. With letters from TA|TE alphabet. 2019

Plakat für das 31. Schaffhauser Jazzfestival 2020.
Mit Buchstaben aus dem Palawan Alphabet. 2019

———

Poster for the 31th Jazzfestival held in Schaffhausen 2020.
With letters of the Palawan alphabet. 2019

Plakat „Weltformat" Graphic Design Festival, Switzerland, Luzern, gestaltet mit Buchstaben des Alphabets Sarawak. 2020

Poster "Weltformat" Graphic Design Festival Switzerland, Lucerne. With letters from the Sarawak alphabet. 2020

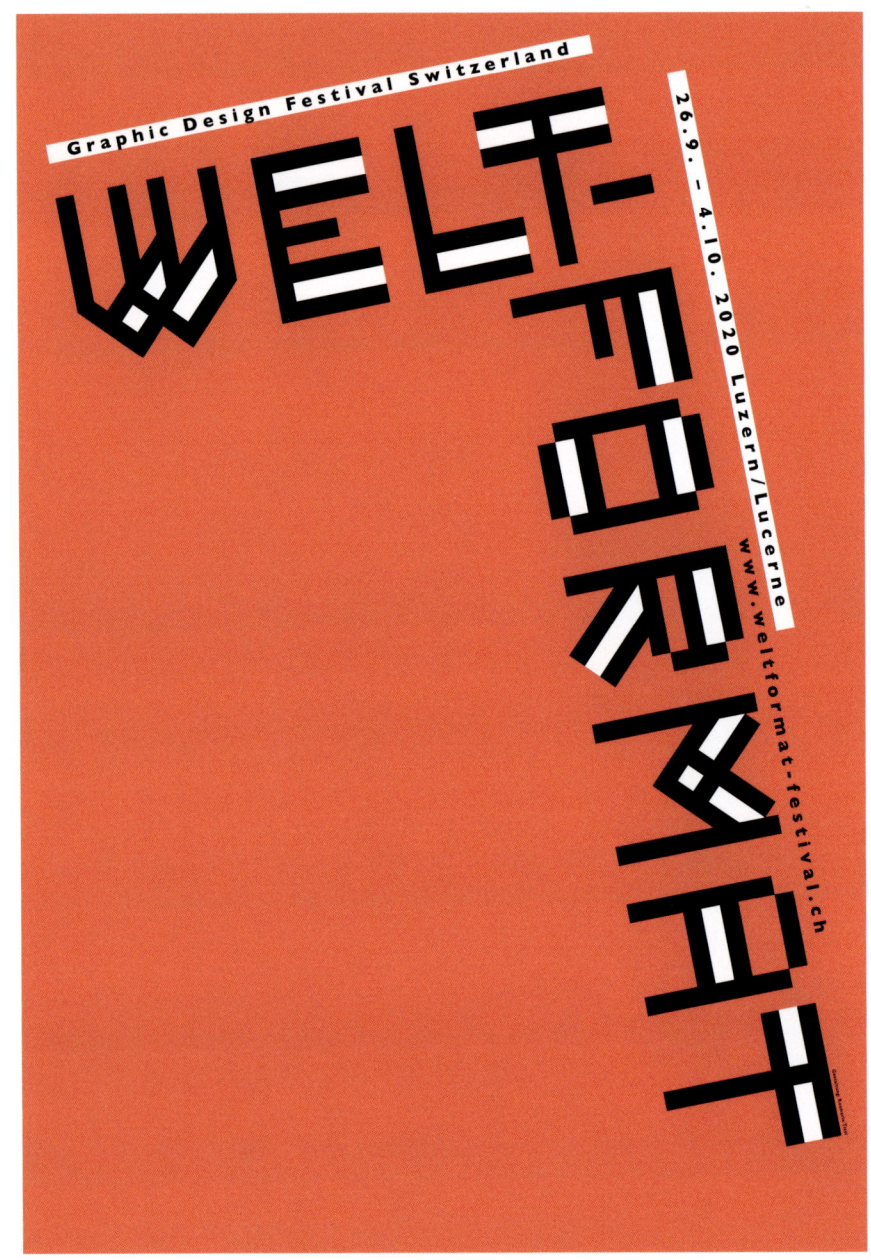

Sarawak 2019

Siladen 2020

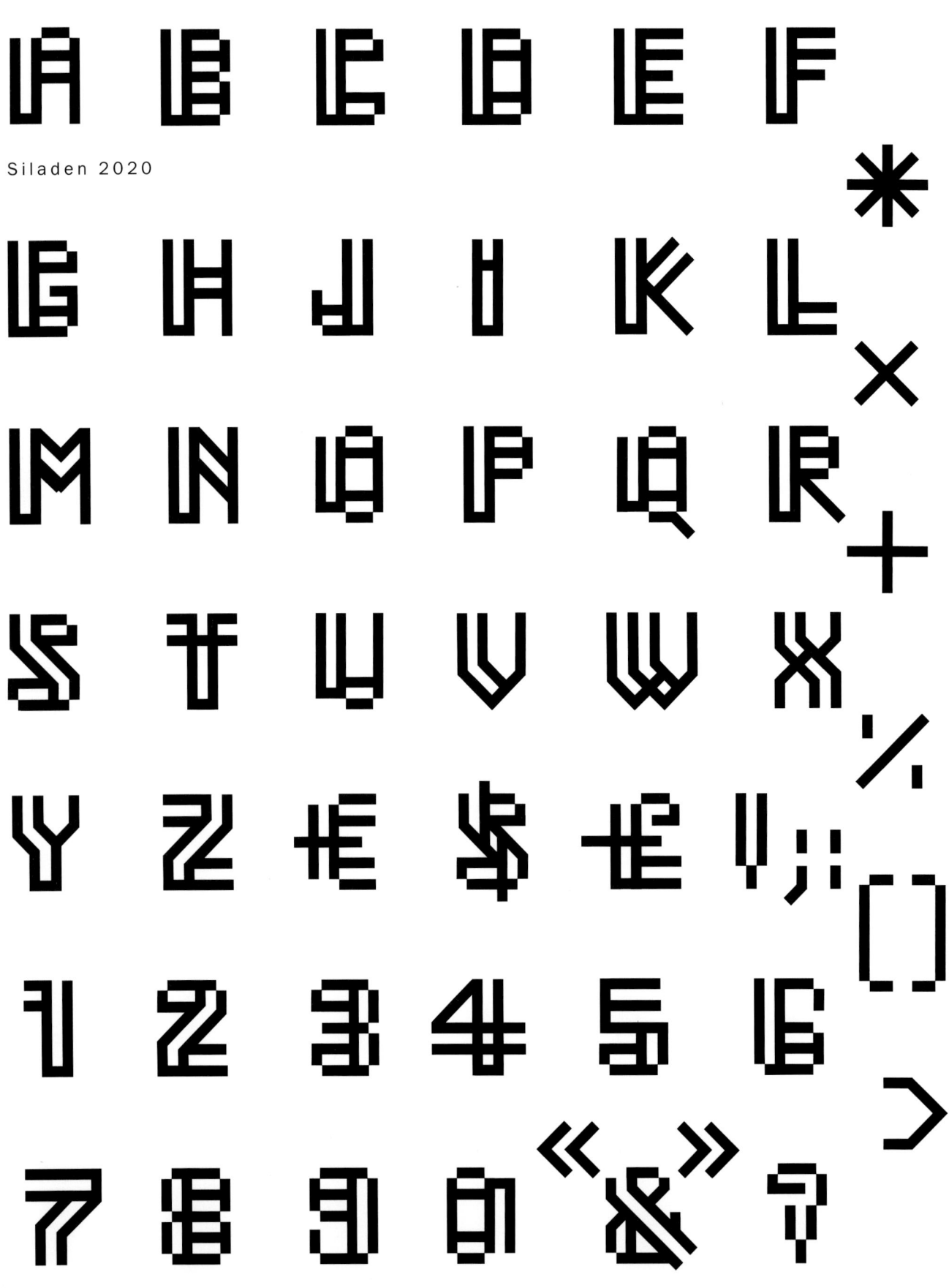

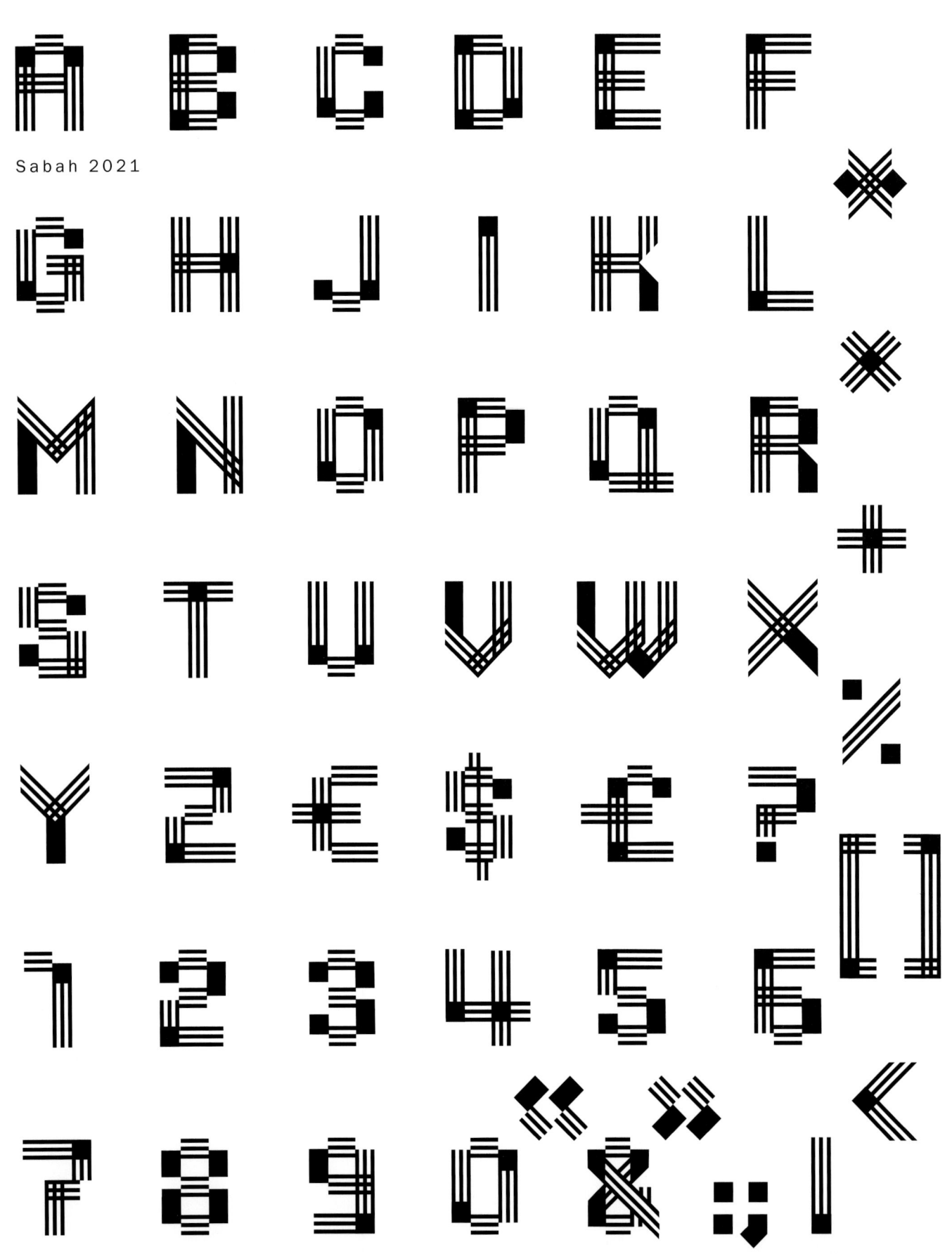

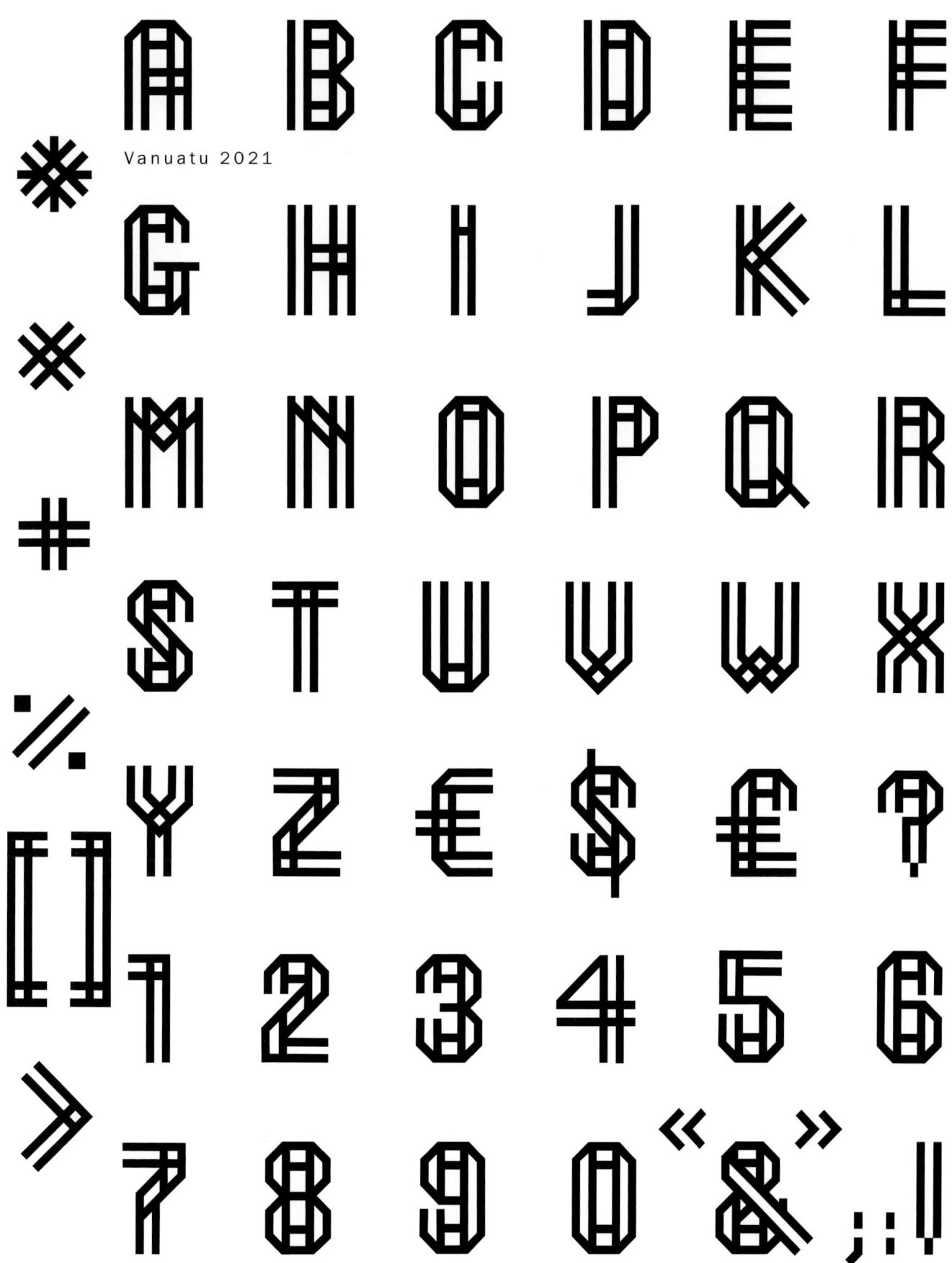

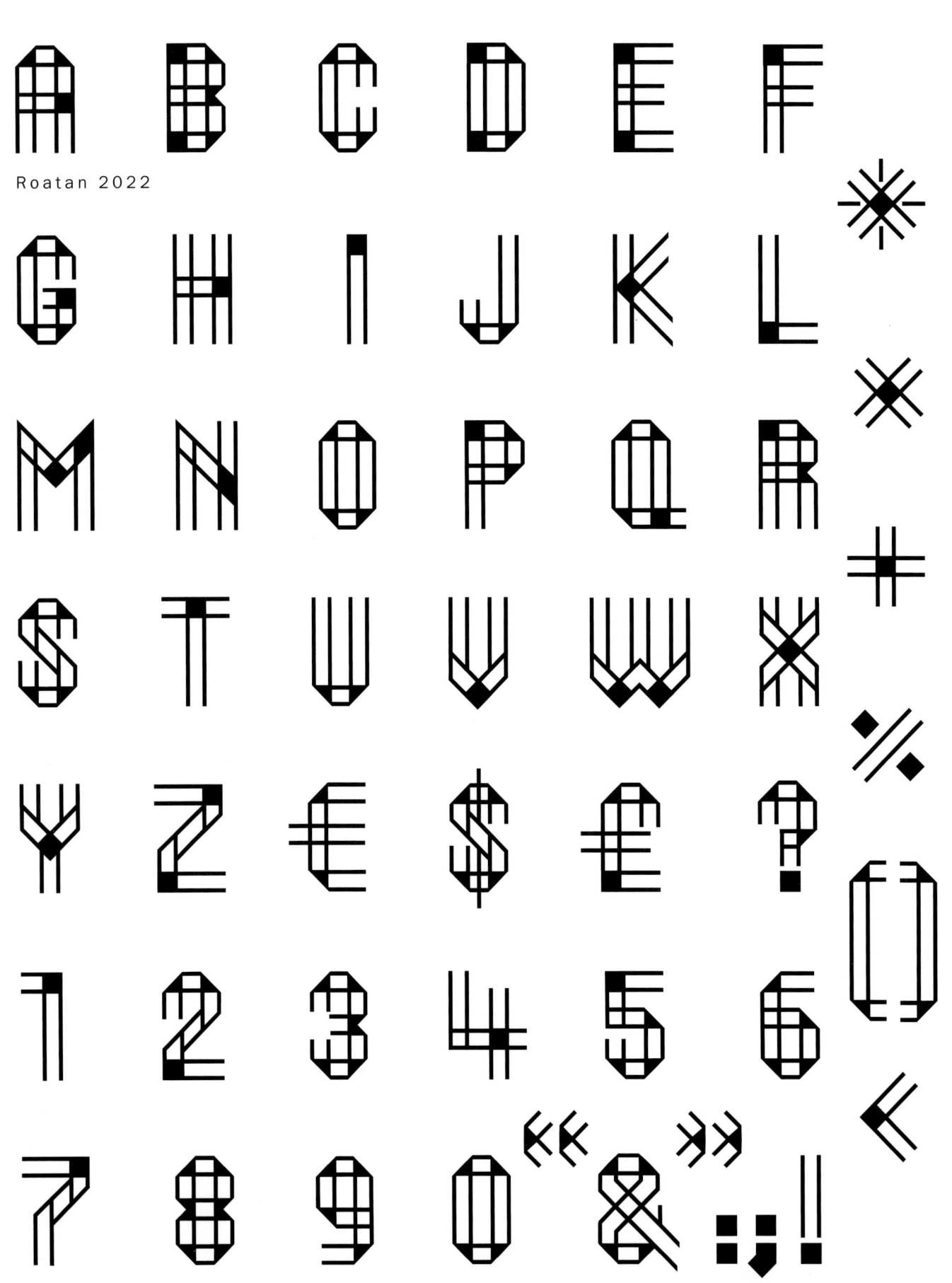

Roatan 2022

Plakat für die Ausstellung „Bulgariens Buchstaben ein Alphabet Europas". Grafiker aus vielen Ländern wurden eingeladen, ein Plakat mit einem Buchstaben zu gestalten. Die Buchstaben, ob kyrillisch oder lateinisch, wurden jedem Designer zugeteilt. 2008

Poster for the exhibition "Bulgarian letters, a European alphabet". Designers from many countries were invited to create a poster with one letter, Cyrillic or Latin. The letters were allocated to each designer. 2008

Neujahrskarte fürs Jahr 2018. Die guten Wünsche werden lesbar unter den zurückgeklappten Quadraten.

New Year's card for 2018. The good wishes are readable under the folded back squares.

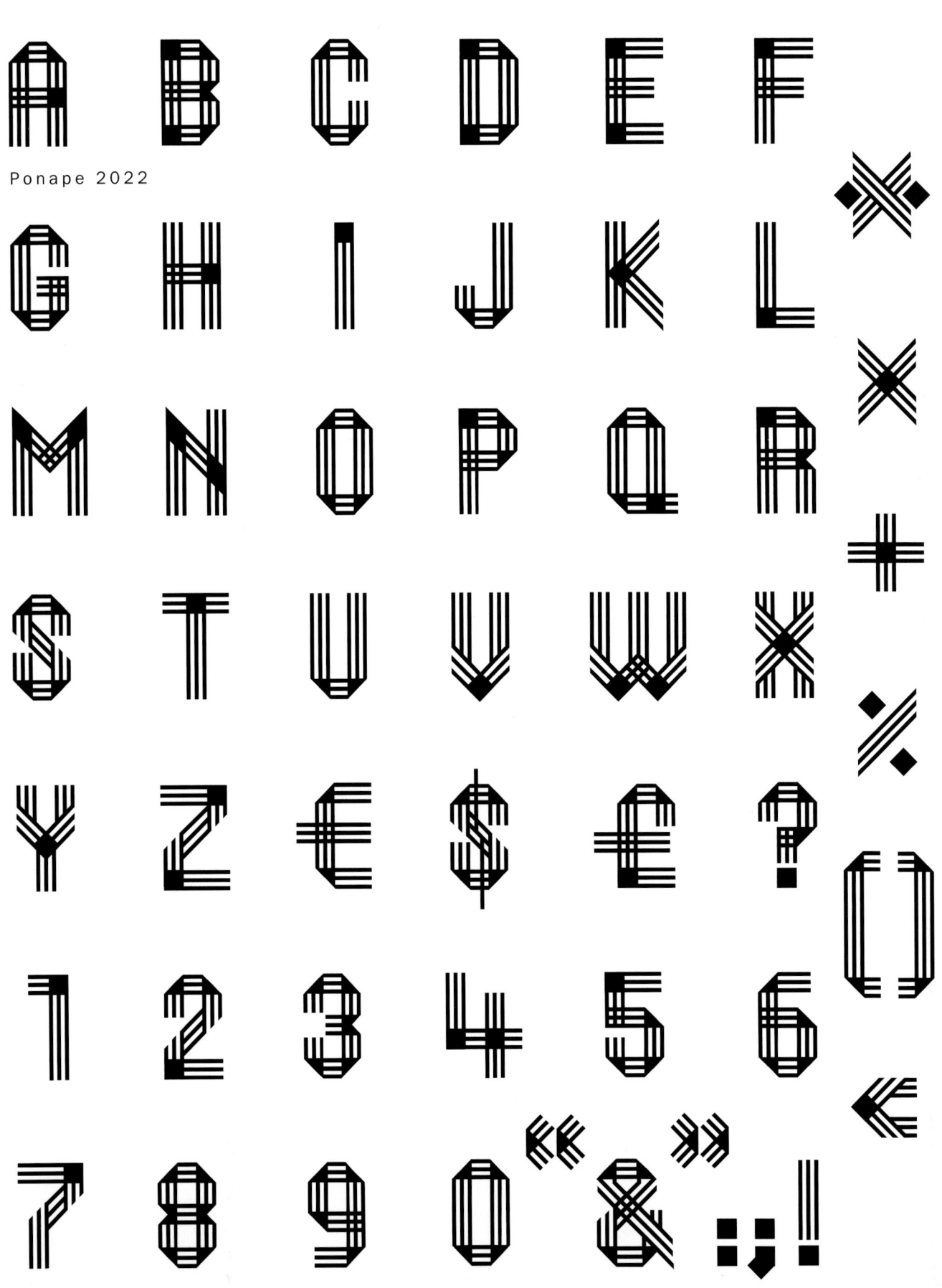

Ponape 2022

2023 hiess das Thema für die Plakat-Safari der Zürcher Design Weeks „Transition". Typografische und farbliche Darstellung von Übergang mit Buchstaben aus den Alphabeten Vanuatu und Ponape.

The theme for the Poster-Safari of the Zurich Design Weeks 2023 was "Transition". The meaning of the word transition is displayed with two different colors and two different typefaces, Vanuatu and Ponape.

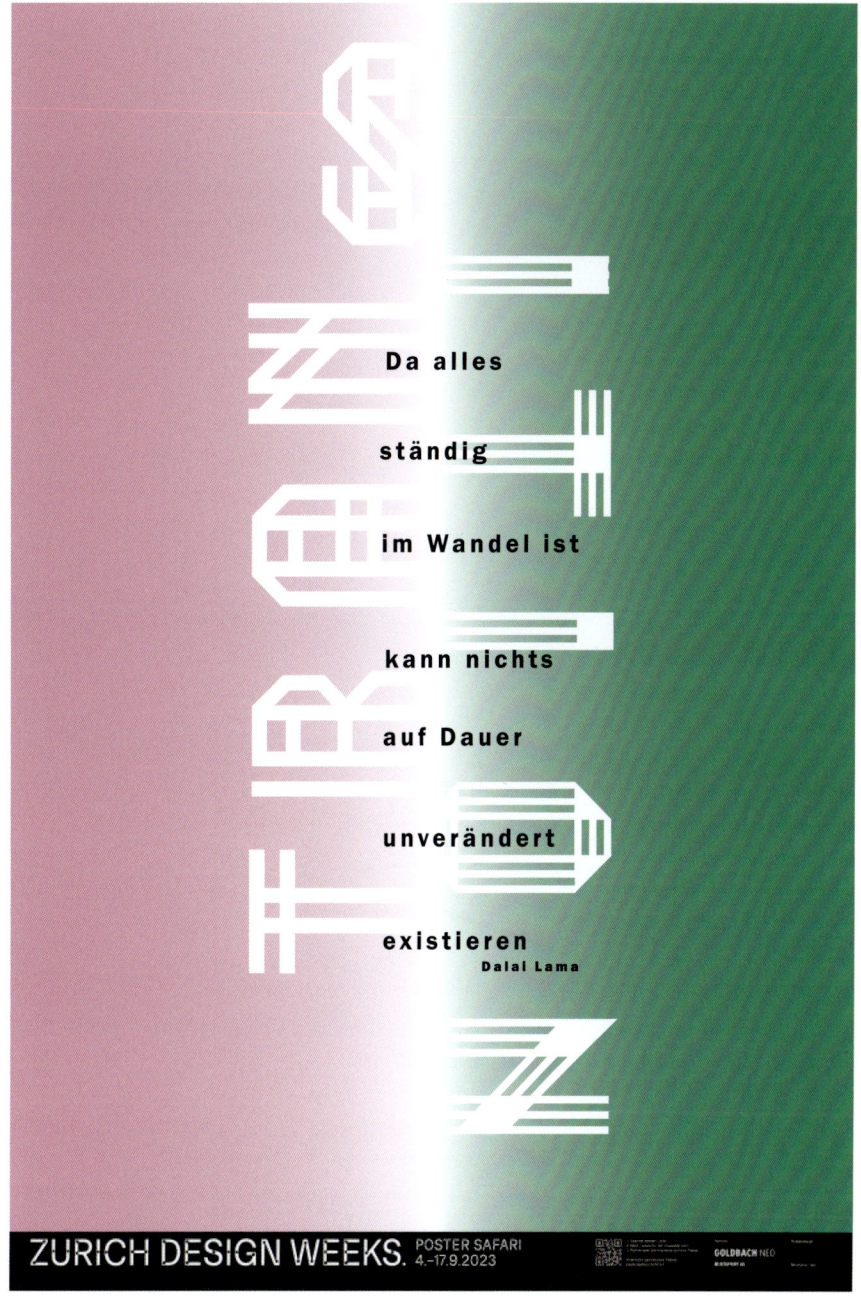

Florian Hardwig über Tissi Type

Rosmarie Tissi hat ihre erste Schrift 1972 entworfen, als freie Arbeit, um die Zeit zwischen Auftragsarbeiten sinnvoll zu nutzen. Ihr Zugang zu Schrift war ein autodidaktischer. Zu anderen Schriftgestaltern hatte sie zu der Zeit keinen Kontakt, Schriftgestalterinnen gab es ohnehin keine. An der Kunstgewerbeschule Zürich erhielt Tissi zwar auch Unterricht in Schrift. Doch der Lehre Walter Kächs konnte sie wenig abgewinnen; die Schreibübungen mit der Redisfeder erschienen ihr veraltet. Ihr Ansatz war ein grafisch-konstruktiver, der auch ihre Arbeit an Plakaten und Signeten bestimmte. Mit Tusche und Deckweiss legte sie die Formen in einer Höhe von etwa fünf Zentimetern fest.

Die Branche war damals im Umbruch begriffen: die Zeiten, in denen ein jeder Gebrauchsgrafiker selbst Schriften zeichnen konnte, waren vorbei. Titelzeilen gab man bei einer der aufkommenden Layoutsetzereien in Auftrag. Diese verfügten über rasch wachsende Kataloge mit Schriften aller Couleur, liessen sich ihre Dienste aber teuer bezahlen. Bei knappem Budget kam Letraset ins Spiel. Ab 1961 sorgte die englische Firma mit Abreibebuchstaben für Aufsehen. Ein Letraset-Bogen war für kleines Geld zu haben und hielt alle Zeichen in einer bestimmten Grösse parat. Das Programm bestand zunächst aus Adaptionen von Standards der Giessereien. Diese wurden bald ergänzt um Originalschriften, die im firmeneigenen Atelier entstanden bzw. bei freiberuflichen Schriftkünstlern beauftragt wurden.

Eine dritte Quelle erschloss Letraset ab 1971 über einen international ausgeschriebenen Wettbewerb. Die von einer hochkarätig (und rein männlich) besetzten Jury ausgewählten Novitäten erschienen in der Letragraphica-Sparte. In diesem auf Profi-Designer abzielenden Modell erhielten Abonnenten vorab Zugang zu den neuesten Schriften. Mit Letragraphica-Ausgabe No. 17 war es soweit. Tissis Einreichung hatte Erfolg, die Sinaloa wurde in drei Grössen (48, 60, 72 Punkt) produziert. Nun war sie weltweit verfügbar – und sofort ein Hit. Bereits Mitte der 1970er Jahre fand sie auf zahlreichen Plattencovern Verwendung. Ein prominentes Beispiel sind die Werke des japanischen Komponisten Isao Tomita. (1) Anders als manch andere Letragraphica-Veröffentlichung, die mangels Nachfrage schon bald wieder aus den Katalogen verschwand, traf die Sinaloa einen Nerv. Sie erfüllte die Anforderungen an eine Displayschrift vollauf: stark und laut, dabei aber so raffiniert, dass sie auch beim zweiten Mal ein Blickfang bleibt.

Formal kombiniert die Sinaloa zwei Eigenschaften, die beide in die Epoche des Art Deco zurückreichen. Zum einen sind da die flächigen Grundformen. Ähnlich geometrisch-blockige Buchstaben, die fast ohne Öffnungen auskommen, finden sich u. a. in italienischen Holzschriften (2) der 1930er Jahre. Zum anderen die parallelen Linien – ein solches Thema kam in der Schriftgestaltung gleichfalls vor einem knappen Jahrhundert auf. Zu den Bleisatzschriften mit solchen Linien zählen Bifur, Prisma und Fatima (3) Sowohl das flächig-geschlossene Moment als auch die Mehrfach-Linien wurden ab Ende der 1960er wieder verstärkt aufgegriffen, jeweils in Kombination mit einer geometrischen Konstruktion. Für ersteres ist die Baby Teeth zu nennen. (4) Für zweiteres spielte sicherlich das Erscheinungsbild der Olympischen Spiele 1968 in Mexiko eine Rolle, für das Lance Wyman eine Linienschrift entwarf. (5) In der Folge erschienen eine ganze Welle von Multiline-Schriften. (6)

Tissis Entwurf vereint beide Eigenschaften auf geniale Weise. Was die Sinaloa auszeichnet, ist die angedeutete Räumlichkeit. In manchen Anwendungen wird das Zusammentreffen der zwei Ebenen durch unterschiedliche Farbgebung hervorgehoben. Ein genauerer Blick auf das Wechselspiel offenbart die geschickte Durcharbeitung: die Linien verlaufen entweder horizontal oder diagonal und strukturieren die Flächen. Mal stellt der Streifenblock einen elementaren Buchstabenteil dar, wie beim Bein des R oder dem Balken des T. Anderenorts, wie in O und W, ist er reine Dekoration, der es der Glyphe aber erlaubt, sich harmonisch in das Gesamtalphabet einzufügen. Dank des variierten Einsatzes der Streifen kommen fast alle Zeichen ohne weitere Einschnitte in die Grundfläche aus. Trotz der formalen Parallelen stellten Schriften wie Bifur keine direkte Inspiration dar; zum Zeitpunkt der Entstehung war Tissi jedenfalls nicht bewusst mit dem Werk Cassandres vertraut. Anders als die zeitgleich entstandenen Alphabete von Marcia Loeb, die sie 1975 als „New Art Deco Alphabets" veröffentlichte (7), kann die Sinaloa nicht als Art-Deco-Schrift bezeichnet werden; sie ist in keiner Weise nostalgisch.

Stilgeschichtlich wurden Tissis Arbeiten gelegentlich mit der Postmoderne in Verbindung gebracht. Die Protagonisten

Florian Hardwig on Tissi Type

Rosmarie Tissi designed her first typeface, Sinaloa, in 1972, as a self-initiated project between clients. She was self-taught in type design; at the time, she had no contact with other type designers, let alone women working in that field – there weren't many yet. Tissi did take courses in lettering at the Zurich School of Arts and Crafts, but she didn't like Walter Käch's teaching very much: the writing exercises with the round-tip pen struck her as outdated. Her approach was a graphical-constructive one, and it also informed her work on posters and logotypes. She used ink and correction fluid to define the letterforms at a height of about five centimeters.

The industry was in a state of flux: the days when the average commercial artist could draw decent letterforms were over. Headlines and other display type were now commissioned from one of the typesetting studios that were cropping up at the time. These had rapidly growing catalogs of typefaces of all kinds, but their services were expensive. When budgets were tighter, Letraset came into play. Starting in 1961, the English company caused a sensation with its dry-transfer product. A Letraset sheet was available for little money and contained all glyphs in a certain size. Letraset's typeface library started with adaptations of foundries' standards. These were soon supplemented by original designs created in-house or commissioned from freelance lettering artists.

Letraset tapped a third source in 1971 through an international competition. The novel designs selected by a high-caliber (and all-male) jury appeared in the Letragraphica range. In this model aimed at professional designers, subscribers were given advance access to the latest releases. With Letragraphica's seventeenth issue, Sinaloa's time had come: Tissi's submission was successful, and produced in three sizes (48, 60, and 72 points). Now Sinaloa was available worldwide – and became an instant hit. By the mid-1970s, it was already being used on numerous record covers. One prominent example is the work of Japanese composer Isao Tomita. (1) Unlike some other Letragraphica releases, which quickly disappeared from catalogs due to lack of demand, Sinaloa struck a nerve. It fully met the requirements of a display typeface: strong and loud, yet refined enough to remain an eye-catcher even the second time around.

On a formal level, Sinaloa combines two features, both of which date back to the art deco era. First, the design is made up of flat basic shapes. Similar geometric, blocky letterforms with little or no apertures and counters can be found in Italian wood type (2) of the 1930s, among other places. The second feature is the parallel lines – this theme emerged in typeface design around the same time. Metal typefaces with such lines include Bifur, Prisma, and Fatima. (3) Both the flat, closed shapes and the multiple lines came back in style from the late 1960s on, typically in combination with a geometric construction. Baby Teeth is a notable example for the first characteristic. (4) For the second, the visual identity of the 1968 Olympic Games in Mexico with Lance Wyman's multiline typeface was influential. (5) In its wake, typefaces made from multiple lines mushroomed. (6)

Tissi's design combines both characteristics in an ingenious way. What distinguishes Sinaloa is its implied spatiality. In some applications, different colors highlighted its two layers. A closer look at the interplay between them reveals the clever execution: the lines run either horizontally or diagonally and structure the shapes. Sometimes the block of stripes represents an elementary part of the letter, as in the leg of R or the bar of T. At other times, as in O and W, it serves as pure decoration, but allows the glyph to blend harmoniously into the overall alphabet. Thanks to the varied use of the stripes, almost all glyphs manage without further incisions in the underlying shape. Despite the formal parallels, typefaces such as Bifur did not represent a direct inspiration; at least at the time of creation, Tissi was not consciously familiar with Cassandre's work. Unlike Marcia Loeb's contemporaneous alphabets, which she published in 1975 as "New Art Deco Alphabets," (7) Sinaloa cannot be described as an Art Deco design; it is in no way nostalgic.

Stylistically, Tissi's work has occasionally been associated with postmodernism. Some protagonists of this movement sought to breathe new life into the constructivism of earlier decades, circumventing old dead ends through shrewd interventions. Indeed, some formal and temporal parallels can be observed. For example, Sinaloa could be read as the typographic equivalent of the style of the Memphis Group around Ettore Sottsass: strictly geometric and at the

1 Tomita: Pictures at an Exhibition, 1975
2 Meneghello & Belluzzo: Etna, 1933
3 A. M. Cassandre: Bifur, 1929; R. Koch: Prisma, 1930; K. H. Schaefer: Fatima, 1933
4 M. Glaser: Baby Teeth, 1966
5 L. Wyman: Mexico 68
6 W. Magin: Black Line, 1969; A. Seki: Aki Lines, 1973
7 M. Loeb: Rainbow, 1975
8 M. De Lucchi: Polar, Kristall, Flamingo, 1981–1984

dieser Richtung versuchten, den Konstruktivismus früherer Jahrzehnte mit neuem Leben zu füllen und dabei alte Sackgassen durch gewitzte Interventionen zu umgehen. In der Tat sind manche formalen und zeitlichen Parallelen zu beobachten. So könnte man die Sinaloa als typografische Entsprechung des Stils der Memphis Group um Ettore Sottsass lesen: streng geometrisch und gleichzeitig wunderbar unverzagt. (8) Doch auch diese Zuschreibung ist nicht gänzlich zutreffend. Tissi selbst sieht sich jedenfalls nicht als Vertreterin der Postmoderne.

Die Wahrnehmung einer Schrift bestimmt nicht die Gestalterin allein. Sie wird von den Assoziationen der Anwender geprägt. Im Fall von Letraset – dem Medium, das die Typografie demokratisierte und auch den Amateuren öffnete – sind diese mannigfaltig.* Das Unkonventionelle der Sinaloa schlägt sich nieder in zahlreichen Anwendungen aus dem Bereich der Musik. Sie reichen von Jazz über Reggae bis Hip-Hop. (9) Selbst auf den Briefkopf des grossen Nonkonformisten Frank Zappa hat sie es geschafft. (10) Dass die Sinaloa inhärent musikalisch ist, legt Rob Stenson mit seiner animierten Hommage nahe: die Streifen interpretiert er als schwingende Gitarrensaiten. (11) Auch bildende Künstler spricht die resolute, freigeistige Ausstrahlung an, wofür exemplarisch eine Installation Ashley Bickertons steht. (12) Ihre Streifen hat die Sinaloa zu einer beliebten Wahl gemacht für alles, was mit Geschwindigkeit zu tun hat, von Transportunternehmen (13) bis hin zu Sportbekleidung. Sicherlich hat Tissi die Linien nicht als „Rallyestreifen" intendiert, und doch fand die Sinaloa den Weg auf ein Rennauto. (14) Nicht wenige Anwender änderten die Buchstabenformen ab. Sie wurden dreidimensional aufgeblasen, kopfstehend eingesetzt oder gänzlich umgezeichnet. Die Streifen wurden verlängert, verkürzt, verlegt und in ihrer Zahl variiert Doch die Sinaloa ist robust. Sie hat einen derart markanten Charakter, dass sie all dies mühelos übersteht. Selbst bei groben Modifikationen bleibt sie stets als Sinaloa erkennbar. Wahrscheinlich ist diese starke, aus zwei an sich simplen Zutaten gespeiste Identität das Geheimnis des Erfolgs.

Letraset gewährte den Entwerfern Tantiemen pro verkauftem Bogen. Besonders hoch können diese nicht gewesen sein – Tissi erinnert sich an eine Zahlung von fünfzig Franken. Angesichts der Verbreitung der Sinaloa ist man

1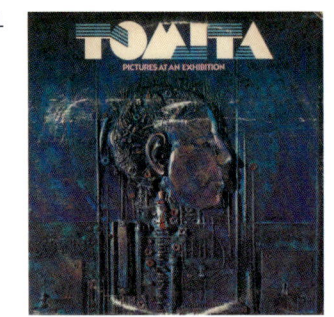

2 AMR

3 ABC ABC ABC

4 ABC

5

6 ABC ABC

7 DECO

8

9   Play-Boys: Reggae Music, 1976 (Daniel)
    Ariel Kalma: Interfrequence, 1980 (B. Eberhard)
    Flyer T-Connection (Detail), 1981
    Beastie Boys: To the 5 Boroughs, 2004

same time wonderfully undaunted. (8) But this attribution is not entirely accurate either. In any case, Tissi does not see herself as a representative of postmodernism.

The perception of a typeface is not determined by its designer alone. It is also shaped by the associations of the user. In the case of Letraset – the medium that democratized typography and opened it up to amateurs – these associations are manifold.* Sinaloa's unconventionality is reflected in numerous applications from the field of music. They range from jazz to reggae to hip-hop. (9) Tissi's typeface even made it onto the letterhead of the great nonconformist that was Frank Zappa. (10) That Sinaloa is inherently musical is suggested by Rob Stenson's animated tribute: he interprets the stripes as vibrating guitar strings. (11) The resolute, free-spirited aura also appeals to visual artists, as an installation by Ashley Bickerton demonstrates. (12) Sinaloa's stripes have made it a popular choice for anything involving speed, from transportation companies (13) to sportswear. Certainly Tissi didn't intend the lines to be "go-faster stripes," and yet Sinaloa found its way onto a race car. (14) Quite a few users altered the letterforms. They were blown up three-dimensionally, turned upside down, or redrawn entirely. Stripes were lengthened, shortened, relocated, and varied in number. But Sinaloa is robust. It has such a distinctive character that it survives all this effortlessly. Even after coarse modifications, it always remains recognizable as Sinaloa. It is probably this strong identity, fed by two simple ingredients, that is the secret to the typeface's success.

Letraset granted the designers royalties per sheet sold. These cannot have been particularly high – Tissi remembers a payment of fifty Swiss francs. Given the proliferation of Sinaloa, one is inclined to doubt the accuracy of the accounting. Of course, there was no payment at all for the pirated copies made by phototypesetting studios. With the advent of the computer, dry-transfer sheets disappeared. Sinaloa, however, remained. As early as 1990, it was distributed in digital form by Letraset. At least five more digitizations exist.** Some of these are anonymous; others came from companies with which Tissi had no ties. Some of them deviate significantly from the original. Two of them added lowercase letters; another, Cyrillic letters. What they all have in common is that they were

9

10 Frank Zappa, ca. 1982
11 R. Stenson: Guitar, 2020
12 A. Bickerton: Me Portrait No 1 (Wildcat), 1987
13 Pangasinan Five Star Bus Company, Philippinen, 2014
14 Citroën BX 4TC, 1986

geneigt, an der Akkuratesse der Abrechnung zu zweifeln. Für die Raubkopien der Fotosatz-Studios gab es natürlich gar keine Vergütung. Mit dem Aufkommen des Computers verschwanden die Abreibe-Bögen. Die Sinaloa aber blieb. Schon 1990 wurde sie von Letraset in digitaler Form vertrieben. Es lassen sich mindestens fünf weitere Digitalisierungen nachweisen.** Teils sind diese anonym, teils stammen sie von Firmen, mit denen Tissi keinerlei Verbindung unterhielt. Manche weichen in den Details deutlich vom Original ab. Zwei erfanden Kleinbuchstaben hinzu, eine andere kyrillische Buchstaben. Was sie alle gemein haben ist, dass sie ohne Autorisierung Tissis gemacht wurden. Eine finanzielle Beteiligung musste die Urheberin sich erst erstreiten. In dieser Hinsicht gibt der Umgang mit der Sinaloa einen traurigen Einblick in das Gebaren vieler Schriftfirmen und ihre oft mangelnde Wertschätzung von Gestaltern. Will man es positiv sehen, so belegt dieses Kapitel die ungebrochene Relevanz der Schrift. Erfreulich ist, dass in Kürze endlich eine autorisierte und technisch hochwertige digitale Fassung erscheinen wird. (LL Sinaloa)

Noch in den 1970ern stellte Tissi zwei weitere Schriften vor. Die Sonora entstand etwa zeitgleich mit der Sinaloa und folgt der selben Grundidee. Hier verlaufen die Streifen durchgehend vertikal, was ihr eine statischere Anmutung verleiht. Die Mindanao von 1975 baut ebenfalls auf blockigen Grundformen auf und betreibt das Spiel mit der räumlichen Wirkung auf eine andere, abermals faszinierende Weise. Hier werden die Zeichen durch Faltkanten definiert. Sie erscheinen als ein- bis vierfach umgeschlagene und isometrisch eingefangene Flächen. Sonora und Mindanao waren ausschliesslich über ein Zürcher Satzstudio verfügbar und kamen folglich zu geringer Verbreitung.***

Nach einer Pause von über dreissig Jahren wandte sich Tissi erneut der Schriftgestaltung zu. 2007 entwarf sie für das Tasse|Teller Projekt der Creation Gallery in Tokio das Wort „ENJOY" und entwickelte später daraus ein komplettes Alphabet. Bis 2010 entstand so die TA|TE. Geometrische Versalien sind aus drei parallelen bzw. bei runden Formen aus vier konzentrischen Linien aufgebaut. Reizvoll sind dabei die Schnittstellen, an denen sich Karos und Rauten bilden. Ausgeführt wurde die TA|TE in zwei Varianten, A und B. Bei ersterer sind ausgewählte Details gefüllt und erzeugen so ein Wechselspiel aus linear und flächig bzw. hell und

15 Z. Licko: Base 9, 1985 / Palawan
16 M. Taut et al.: Verbandshaus der Deutschen Buchdrucker, Berlin, 1924–1926 / Siladen
17 Red and White Menzies Tartan, vor 1500 / R. P. Lohse: Plakat, 1961, © 2024, ProLitteris, Zurich / Sabah
18 P. Mondrian: Broadway Boogie Woogie (Detail), 1943 / Roatan
19 M. Bill: Plakat (Detail), 1976, © 2024, ProLitteris, Zurich / Lombok
20 B. Bodhuin: Mineral, 2013 / Vanuatu
21 Giuda: Tourplakat (Detail), 2023

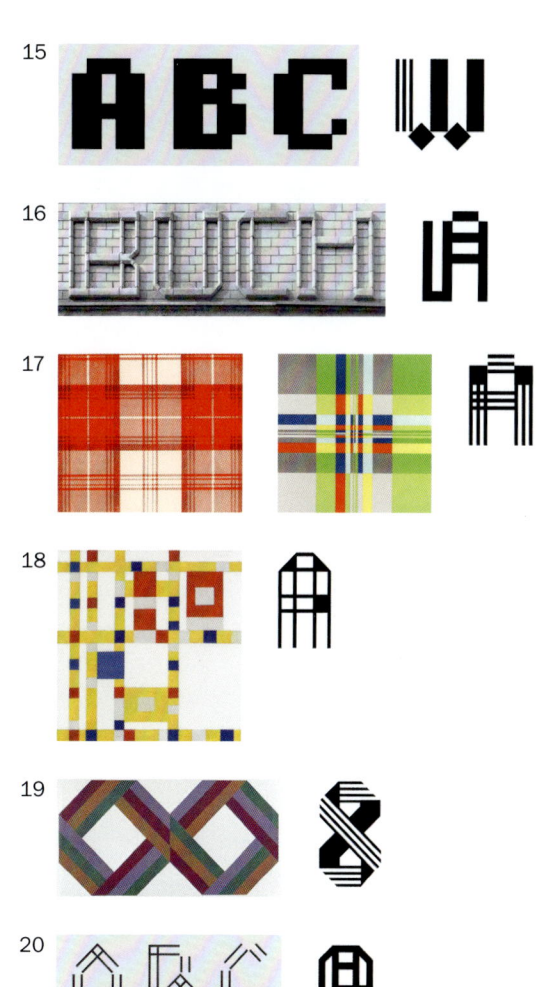

made without Tissi's authorization. She had to fight for financial compensation. In this respect, the way Sinaloa was handled provides us sad insight into the conduct of many type companies and their lack of appreciation for designers. In a more positive light, this chapter is proof of the typeface's continued relevance. It is gratifying to learn that, at last, an authorized and high-quality digitization will soon be available. (LL Sinaloa)

Tissi introduced two other typefaces in the 1970s. Sonora was created around the same time as Sinaloa and follows the same basic idea. Here, the stripes run vertically throughout, which produces a more static appearance. Mindanao, from 1975, is likewise based on blocky basic forms and plays with the spatial effect in a different, yet again fascinating way. Here the glyphs are defined by folded edges. They appear as surfaces folded over one to four times and captured isometrically. Sonora and Mindanao were available exclusively through a Zurich typesetting studio and consequently received scant circulation***.

After a hiatus of more than thirty years, Tissi once again turned to type design. Starting from a wordmark created in 2007, she developed a complete alphabet. By 2010, this had led to TA|TE. Geometric capitals are made up of three parallel lines or, in the case of round shapes, four concentric lines. The appeal lies in the intersections that yield checkered patterns. TA|TE was executed in two variants, A and B. In the former, selected details are filled, creating an interplay of linear and planar, or light and dark. Palawan, from 2014, has a similar motif. Here, Tissi limits herself to verticals, horizontals, and diagonals, trying to find an appealing solution for all the glyphs within the given framework. The stepped forms are reminiscent of early screen fonts. Nevertheless, the typeface has little in common with the bitmap fonts of her peer Zuzana Licko. (15) Tissi counteracts a pixel (anti)aesthetic by interspersing diagonal elements that break the grid and are more reminiscent of miniatures made of building blocks. The numerals, some of which are based on octagonal forms, bring the numbers on sports jerseys to mind – an association that is further reinforced by the stripes.

Starting in 2019, Tissi created seven new alphabets in rapid succession. Like the earlier typefaces, they are all-caps

dunkel. Die Palawan von 2014 hat ein ähnliches Motiv. Hier beschränkt sich Tissi auf Vertikale, Horizontale und Diagonale und versucht, innerhalb dieses Rahmens für alle Zeichen eine ansprechende Lösung zu finden. Die getreppten Formen lassen dabei an frühe Bildschirmschriften denken. Mit den Bitmapfonts ihrer Kollegin Zuzana Licko hat die Schrift dennoch wenig gemein. (15) Eine Pixel(anti)ästhetik konterkariert Tissi durch Einstreuen diagonaler Elemente, welche das Raster sprengen und eher an aus Bausteinen gelegte Miniaturen erinnern. Bei den teils auf achteckigen Hochkantformen beruhenden Ziffern hat man wiederum die Nummern von Sporttrikots vor Augen – eine Assoziation, die durch die Streifen noch verstärkt wird.

Ab 2019 entstanden in rascher Folge gleich sieben neue Alphabete. Sie sind wie die früheren Schriften allesamt rein versal und, anders als diese, eher schmal gehalten. Bei der Sarawak blitzt erneut die Bitmap-Anmutung auf. Gleichzeitig haben Zeichen mit schrägen Strichen etwas Runenhaftes. Hier besteht die „Spielregel" darin, alle Zeichen mit Strichstärkenkontrast auszustatten. Die Verteilung von dick und dünn folgt dabei bewusst nicht der vom Schreibwerkzeug abgeleiteten Konvention. Mal sind es die Horizontalen, mal die Diagonalen, auf denen die Betonung liegt. Und wo sich weder das eine noch das andere anbietet, wird – wie beim P – das Gewicht kurzerhand in die Innenform verlegt, um die Idee durchzuhalten. Durch Zweifarbigkeit gewinnt die Sarawak an Körperlichkeit, wie es Tissi in ihrer eigenen Anwendung vorführt. Die Siladen changiert ganz ähnlich zwischen offenen und geschlossenen Formen sowie technoider und archaischer Ausstrahlung. Mit ihren gerahmten Strichen und der ausgeprägten Vertikalität hat sie zudem etwas von architektonischen Schriften der 1920er. (16) In der aus Dreifach-Linien aufgebauten Sabah sind Überschneidungen das bestimmende Thema. Wo die Streifen aufeinandertreffen und sich verdichten, ist der Gedanke an Textilmuster schottischer Clans nicht weit; ebenso die konkrete Kunst eines Richard Paul Lohse. (17)

Die vier jüngsten Schriften – Vanuatu, Lombok, Roatan und Ponape – können als Serie gelesen werden. Sie weisen ähnlich schmale Proportionen und weitgehend identische Grundformen auf. Während die Vanuatu die starken Linien von Sarawak und Siladen aufgreift, rekurriert die Ponape auf das von TA|TE und Sabah bekannte „textile" Element.

Die Roatan mit ihren feinen Linien und akzentuierten Schnittpunkten scheint geradewegs dem Broadway Boogie Woogie Piet Mondrians entsprungen zu sein. (18) Die Lombok wiederum offenbart die persönliche Bekanntschaft und stilistische Verwandtschaft mit Max Bill. (19) Manche Zeichen erscheinen wie akkurat gefaltete Bänder mit unterschiedlich gefärbten Seiten. Mit ihr kehrt Tissi zurück zu den horizontal und diagonal verlaufenden Streifen der Sinaloa. Was sich durch alle Entwürfe zieht, ist das Ausloten des Punktes zwischen zu wenig und zu viel. Eine jede Glyphe ist eine grafische Miniatur, die zugleich im System des Alphabets funktionieren muss. Tissis Herangehensweise ist dabei minimalistisch, nicht aber simplistisch. So ist etwa das W nie einfach nur ein kopfstehendes M. Wenn ein Zeichen nicht funktioniert – Tissi nennt das S als Knackpunkt – dann ist die ganze Idee hinfällig. Die Ergebnisse sind durchaus als zeitgenössisch zu beschreiben: es sind interessante Parallelen zu Arbeiten jüngerer Gestalter zu beobachten, vgl. etwa Vanuatu und Mineral von Benoît Bodhuin (20)

Die neuen Schriften müssen sich hinsichtlich ihrer Verwendbarkeit erst noch beweisen. Bislang kamen sie lediglich in eigenen Arbeiten Tissis zum Einsatz, und auch dort meist als einzelne, teils dekonstruierte Zeichen. Ganz unabhängig von ihrer Qualität werden Ponape & Co. nicht die unmittelbare und weitreichende Verbreitung finden, die die Sinaloa erfahren hat. Der Schriftmarkt ist heute ein anderer; das Angebot um ein Vielfaches grösser und der Vertrieb kleinteiliger. Die Sinaloa aber ist nach wie vor beliebt und wirkmächtig. (21) Sie traf den Zeitgeist der 1970er Jahre und hat auch heute, ein halbes Jahrhundert nach ihrer Entstehung ihre Gültigkeit. Mit ihr hat Rosmarie Tissi einen wahren Klassiker geschaffen.

* Tissi hat nie Letraset verwendet.
** Freiere Interpretationen sind da nicht mitgezählt – wie jene, welche die Sinaloa durchaus humorvoll mit einem weiteren Letraset-Klassiker, der Frankfurter, zur „Sinafurter" hybridisiert.
*** Die Schriften sind auch in Katalogen der Stuttgarter Layout-Setzerei Stulle gelistet, inklusive einer offenen Variante der Mindanao, die hier Namibia heisst.

only, but, unlike those, of rather narrow proportions. In Sarawak, the bitmap impression once again shines through. At the same time, the glyphs with diagonals have something runic about them. Here, the rule of the game is to provide all glyphs with stroke-width contrast. The distribution of thick and thin deliberately does not follow the convention derived from writing tools. Sometimes emphasis is placed on the horizontals, other times on the diagonals. And where neither one nor the other lends itself to being emphasized, the weight is unceremoniously shifted to the inner form – as in the case of the P – to keep the idea alive. In bichromatic use, Sarawak gains physicality, as Tissi demonstrates in her own application. Siladen similarly oscillates between open and closed forms, between technoid and archaic appeal. With its framed strokes and pronounced verticality, it also has something of 1920s architectural typefaces. (16) In Sabah, which is constructed of triple lines, intersections are the defining theme. Where the stripes meet and densify, the thought of Scottish tartan patterns is not far-fetched; neither is the concrete art of Richard Paul Lohse. (17)

The four most recent alphabets – Vanuatu, Lombok, Roatan and Ponape – can be regarded as a series. They have similar narrow proportions and largely identical basic forms. While Vanuatu takes up the thick lines of Sarawak and Siladen, Ponape resorts to the "textile" element familiar from TA|TE and Sabah. Roatan, with its fine lines and accentuated intersections, seems to have sprung straight from Piet Mondrian's Broadway Boogie Woogie. (18) Lombok, in turn, reveals Tissi's personal acquaintance and stylistic affinity with Max Bill. (19) Some glyphs look like accurately folded ribbons with different-colored sides. With Lobok, Tissi returns to the horizontal and diagonal stripes of Sinaloa. What runs through all the designs is the fathoming of the point between too little and too much. Each glyph is a graphic miniature that at the same time must function within the system of the alphabet. Tissi's approach is minimalist, but not simplistic. The W, for example, is never simply an upside-down M. If one glyph doesn't work – Tissi cites the S as a sticking point – then the whole idea is invalid. The results can certainly be described as contemporary: interesting parallels to works by younger designers can be observed; compare, for example, Vanuatu to Benoît Bodhuin's Mineral. (20)

The new alphabets have yet to prove their usability. So far, they have only appeared in Tissi's own works, and even there mostly as individual, partly deconstructed glyphs. Regardless of their quality, Ponape and company will not find the immediate and widespread distribution that Sinaloa experienced. The font market is different today; supply is many times larger and distribution is more fragmented. But Sinaloa is still a popular and effective design. (21) It tapped the zeitgeist of the 1970s and remains valid today, half a century after its creation. With Sinola, Rosmarie Tissi created a true classic.

* Tissi herself never used Letraset.
** Freer interpretations are not included in that number – such as the one that, quite humorously, hybridizes Sinaloa with another Letraset classic, Frankfurter, to form "Sinafurter."
*** The typefaces are also listed in catalogs of the Stuttgart typesetting company Stulle, including an open variant of Mindanao, which is called Namibia here.

Encounters with Rosmarie Tissi
Paula Scher, Partner at Pentagram New York

Begegnungen mit Rosmarie Tissi

I was first aware of Rosmarie Tissi's work in the mid-80s. I didn't know she was a woman. The work I saw then was credited as Odermatt & Tissi which was the name of her office in Switzerland. Odermatt & Tissi were partners but, I made the assumption that they were both men. because all of the Swiss designers I knew about at that time were men, as were almost all of the designers that I knew about everywhere. Then one day in a design annual or magazine I saw a specific piece of her work which I had already admired and it was credited to Rosmarie Tissi. "Rosmarie" – a woman!

Her work was, and still is, elegant and powerful, analytical and intuitive, modern and post-modern, all at once. While reflecting on her now, I Googled her work to remind myself of what I had admired about it, and discovered that it is still fresh and incontrived. The contradictions in her work keep it from dating.

I met Rosmarie in Camden, Maine in the late'80s when a select group of mostly luddite designers were invited to a seminar that introduced us to the Macintosh and were we learned to operate Photoshop and other programs. We both hated it, to the point of tears. We felt like it inhibited our creativity and we bonded through the experience. Later, however, Rosmarie mastered it; I never did.

After that, we saw each other several times at annual AGI conferences in the early'90s, where we were both early woman members in an organization that was slow to accept them. And, in the late'90s we saw each other in Tehran, Iran where we were part of a group of international designers invited to exhibit posters at the Tehran Museum of Modern Art. It was a highly memorable and interesting trip, but both of us resented being forced to wear the headscarf publicly every day. It offended us deeply. It damaged our self-images much more than either of us had ever anticipated, and, of course, that is its desired effect. The men in our group had no such dictate.

Rosmarie and I haven't seen each other in years but I always look forward to her spectacular New Years cards that seem to be indvidually crafted and are gecognizable without her signature. I imagine she hasn't changed much in spirit. Neither have I.

Ich begegnete Rosmarie Tissis Arbeiten zum ersten Mal Mitte der 1980er Jahre. Dass sie eine Frau ist, wusste ich nicht. Die Arbeit, die ich damals sah, war Odermatt & Tissi zugeschrieben, was der Name ihres Ateliers in der Schweiz war. Odermatt & Tissi waren Partner, aber ich ging davon aus, dass es sich um Männer handelte, weil es sich bei allen mir damals bekannten Schweizer Designern um Männer handelte, und nicht nur bei den Schweizer Designern. Dann sah ich eines Tages in einem Jahrbuch oder Magazin eine spezielle Arbeit, die ich schon bewundert hatte, und diese Arbeit war Rosmarie Tissi zugeschrieben. „Rosmarie" – eine Frau!

Ihre Arbeit war, und ist es noch, elegant und kraftvoll, analytisch und intuitiv, modern und postmodern, alles auf einmal. Als ich mich jetzt wieder mit ihr befasste, googelte ich ihre Arbeiten, um mich an das zu erinnern, was mich so beeindruckt hatte, und ich stellte fest, dass ihre Arbeiten noch immer frisch und ungekünstelt sind. Ihre Arbeiten altern nicht, dank der erwähnten Gegensätze.

Ich traf Rosmarie in Camden, Maine, in den späten 80er Jahren, als eine ausgesuchte Gruppe extrem skeptischer Designer zu einem Seminar geladen war, in dem wir mit dem Macintosh sowie der Arbeit mit Photoshop und anderen Programmen vertraut gemacht werden sollten. Beide hassten wir diese Technologie und waren den Tränen nahe. Wir sahen unsere Kreativität gefährdet, und diese Erfahrung verband uns. Später jedoch lernte Rosmarie damit umzugehen, was ich nie tat.

Danach sahen wir uns wiederholt an AGI-Konferenzen in den frühen 90er Jahren. Wir gehörten zu den ersten weiblichen Mitgliedern in einer Organisation, die Frauen nur zögerlich akzeptierte. In den späten 90er Jahren begegneten wir uns in Teheran wieder. Wir gehörten zu einer Gruppe internationaler Designer, die eingeladen waren, Plakate im Museum of Modern Art in Teheran auszustellen. Es war ein sehr eindrucksvoller und interessanter Aufenthalt, aber beide waren wir verärgert, dass wir gezwungen waren, jeden Tag in der Öffentlichkeit das Kopftuch zu tragen. Es verletzte uns zutiefst. Wir hatten nicht damit gerechnet, dass es unser Selbstverständnis derart beeinträchtigen würde, was natürlich genau der gewünscte Effekt ist. Die Männer in unserer Gruppe blieben von Vorschriften unbehelligt.

Rosmarie und ich haben uns jahrelang nicht gesehen, aber ich freue mich immer auf ihre spektakulären Neujahrskarten, die sie offenbar einzeln anfertigt. Man erkennt sie sofort, auch ohne ihre Signatur. Ich nehme an, sie hat sich nicht verändert – ich auch nicht.

Bildnachweis / Picture Credits

1 Internet Archive https://archive.org/details/lp_pictures-at-an-exhibition_tomita
8 Design Museum https://designmuseum.org/discover-design/all-stories/memphis-group-awful-or-awesome
9a Discogs https://www.discogs.com/release/5094132-Play-Boys-Reggae-Music
9b Black Sweat Records https://blacksweat.bandcamp.com/album/interfrequence
9c Johan Kugelberg hip hop collection, #8021. Division of Rare and Manuscript Collections, Cornell University Library. https://digital.library.cornell.edu/catalog/ss:1334137
9d Internet Archive https://archive.org/details/cd_to-the-5-boroughs_beastie-boys
10 Kill Ugly Radio https://www.killuglyradio.com/2010/01/19/frank-zappa%E2%80%99s-original-pmrc-letters/
11 Rob Stenson https://twitter.com/robstenson/status/1215433090962640896
12 Leo Reynolds https://www.flickr.com/photos/lwr/45164798414/
13 Judgefloro https://commons.wikimedia.org/wiki/File:FvfTayugPangasinan5367_42.JPG
14 MIMI3163 http://forum-auto.caradisiac.com/automobile-pratique/modelisme-modeles-reduits/sujet12126-525.htm
16 Florian Hardwig https://www.flickr.com/photos/hardwig/8475234653/
17b Zürcher Hochschule der Künste / Museum für Gestaltung Zürich / Plakatsammlung https://www.emuseum.ch/de/objects/14627/ohne-text
18a https://en.wikipedia.org/wiki/Broadway_Boogie_Woogie#/media/File:Piet_Mondrian,_1942_-_Broadway_Boogie_Woogie.jpg
19a Zürcher Hochschule der Künste / Museum für Gestaltung Zürich / Plakatsammlung https://www.emuseum.ch/de/objects/70902/akademie-der-kunste--max-bill?ctx=93bb526cd1eeccb1fa520bc442ef1b92ba29e261&idx=1
21 Giuda https://www.facebook.com/giudaofficial/posts/pfbid02x69qrJskrfJMWZpL86f6TAZQ4xY8Mv5LdUVpt-WoqguLCvJemgyMr6H8J1tpGMGz2l?locale=de_DE

Impressum / Imprint

Herausgeberin / Editor: Rosmarie Tissi
Gestaltung / Design: Rosmarie Tissi und Bruno Margreth
Texte / Texts: Herbert Lechner, Florian Hardwig,
Paula Scher
Druck / Printing: Offizin Scheufele, Stuttgart
Buchbindung / Book binding: Gert Schallenmüller, Stuttgart

About Books GmbH
Flurstrasse 93
CH-8047 Zürich
www.aboutbooks.ch

1. Auflage / First edition 2024
ISBN 978-3-906946-38-2

© 2024 Rosmarie Tissi & About Books

Herausgeberin und Verlag haben sich bemüht, alle Inhaber:innen von Urheberrechten ausfindig zu machen. Sollten dabei Fehler oder Auslassungen unterlaufen sein, werden diese bei entsprechender Benachrichtigung in der folgenden Auflage korrigiert. Etwaige Rechteinhaber:innen möchten sich bitte mit dem entsprechenden Nachweis an den Verlag wenden.
Despite best efforts, we have not been able to identify the holders of copyright and printing rights for all the illustrations in this book. Copyright holders not mentioned in the credits are asked to substantiate their claims, and recompense will be made according to standard practice.

Alle Rechte vorbehalten; kein Teil dieses Werkes darf in irgendeiner Form ohne vorherige schriftliche Genehmigung des Verlags reproduziert oder unter Verwendung elektronischer Systeme verarbeitet, vervielfältigt oder verbreitet werden.
All rights reserved; no part of this publication may be reproduced, stored in a retrieval system or transmitted in any form or by any means, electronic, mechanical, photocopying, recording, or otherwise, without the prior written consent of the publisher.

Herzlichen Dank allen, die zum guten Gelingen dieser Publikation beigetragen haben:
Many thanks to all who contributed to the success of this publication:

Céline Odermatt
Cornel Windlin
Phillip Niemeyer
Noa Bacchetta
Heinke Jenssen

Diese Publikation wurde unterstützt durch:
This publication has been realized with the kind support of:

Gemeinde Thayngen
Kulturverein Thayngen Reiat
Martin Huber-Tissi

JAKOB UND EMMA
WINDLER-STIFTUNG